"Kyle Idleman is rock solid. He loves the Bible, loves people, and loves to teach people the Bible. If you read this book, you can expect to be encouraged, challenged, and better because of it."

Max Lucado, *New York Times* bestselling author

"Kyle has written yet another terrific book. He reminds us about the power of presence and taking a genuine interest in the person right in front of us rather than being distracted by the many other shiny things around us. It isn't new math to influence a few more people that you will find in these pages but a reminder of the old math Jesus used to change the entire world."

Bob Goff, author of *New York Times* bestsellers *Love Does, Everybody Always*, and *Dream Big*

"As Christians, we want our lives to matter, to count for something. We may be tempted to measure our efforts by numbers, but Jesus was clearly focused on one person at a time. If we really want to be faithful followers of Christ, we need to follow his example. In this book, Kyle Idleman will help you see yourself as a true influencer and identify how to change the world *One at a Time*."

Craig Groeschel, pastor of Life Church and *New York Times* bestselling author

"I have been blown away by Kyle Idleman's kindness and support. This book helped me understand the source of his kindness and support: he was just following Jesus. The truths in the chapters ahead are both revolutionary and simple. This book is going to change Christians, one at a time."

Jonathan "JP" Pokluda, pastor of Harris Creek and bestselling author

"*One at a Time* is a deeply personal book written for the hands and feet of Jesus—his followers. We are the ones called to share, serve, and sacrifice. We are the anointed empowered to care for others. In this encouragement, Kyle Idleman is realistic: we cannot do everything for everyone, but we can be there for one another one at a time. He shows us how."

Mark Batterson, *New York Times* bestselling author of *The Circle Maker* and lead pastor of National Community Church

"Kyle Idleman is a fresh and powerful voice for faith in our time. With clarity and insight, *One at a Time* shows how you can change the world and have a meaningful impact."

Jud Wilhite, senior pastor of Central Church
and author of *Uncaged*

"Do you want to make a big impact with your life? Then go small! Try focusing your attention and activities on one person whom God wants you to reach for him—and watch what happens. After all, revivals start one individual at a time. In this practical and entertaining guide, my friend Kyle Idleman will inspire and equip you to take the path blazed by Jesus himself. Whatever you do, don't miss the adventure that awaits you!"

Lee Strobel, founding director, Strobel Center for Evangelism
and Applied Apologetics at Colorado Christian University

"*One at a Time* is the way of Jesus, so it should be our practice as well. Kyle Idleman shares this compelling insight with persuasive stories from the Scriptures and modern life. Whether we are called to disciple a questioning follower, rescue an unwanted child, or care for a needy neighbor, we can only do it one by one. In the name of Jesus, read this book and minister to others one at a time."

Roland Warren, president and CEO of Care Net and author
of *Raising Sons of Promise*

"A few years ago, I was backstage after finishing up an event in Louisville. I'd recently recovered from an illness, and I was sitting alone with my own thoughts when Kyle walked up. He asked how I was feeling and how my family was doing, and our conversation lasted twenty or thirty minutes. I was deeply encouraged and spurred on by our chat, and I've never forgotten it. As I was reading Kyle's new book, I was struck that before this book ever existed, he was living this 'one at a time' mantra, and in that moment backstage, I was the one he was impacting and influencing. I was the one."

Luke Smallbone, For King & Country

"*One at a Time* is a unique roadmap to influence. It is a testimony of a church transformed and a pastor molded by Jesus's passion to see people in the crowd, not crowds of people. Do you want to be influential? *One at a Time* is your template."

Mark E. Moore, PhD, author of *Core 52* and teaching pastor
at Christ's Church of the Valley

one
at a time

one
at a time

the unexpected way
God wants to use you
to change the world

kyle idleman

BakerBooks
a division of Baker Publishing Group
www.BakerBooks.com

Published by Baker Books
a division of Baker Publishing Group
PO Box 6287, Grand Rapids, MI 49516-6287
www.bakerbooks.com

Printed in the United States of America

Library of Congress Cataloging-in-Publication Data
Names: Idleman, Kyle, author.
Title: One at a time : the unexpected way God wants to use you to change the world / Kyle Idleman.
Description: Grand Rapids, MI : Baker Books, a division of Baker Publishing Group, [2022] |
Identifiers: LCCN 2021020367 | ISBN 9780801094910 (paperback) | ISBN 9781540902078 (casebound) | ISBN 9781493433940 (ebook)
Subjects: LCSH: Christian life. | Change—Religious aspects—Christianity. | Jesus Christ—Example. | Interpersonal relations—Religious aspects—Christianity.
Classification: LCC BV4501.3 .I36 2022 | DDC 248.4—dc23
LC record available at https://lccn.loc.gov/2021020367

Published in association with the literary agent Don Gates of The Gates Group, www.the-gates-group.com.

Baker Publishing Group publications use paper produced from sustainable forestry practices and post-consumer waste whenever possible.

22 23 24 25 26 27 28   7 6 5 4 3 2 1

To Christina and Kawandah:
you didn't know me but you knew Jesus,
and you loved people one at a time—
and then one day, at just the right time,
one of the people you loved happened to be one
of the most important people in the world to me.
Thank you for loving one at a time.

introduction

I DON'T KNOW of any person who doesn't want to make a difference in the world.

Nobody grows up dreaming of waking up, going to work, heading home, watching Netflix, scrolling through social media, and then doing it all over again the next day until their last breath. We all want to be used to change the world.

We don't want to spend our lives being time-wasters, or space-takers, or binge-watchers, or game-players, or even book-readers. We want to be difference-makers. And my guess is the reason you picked up this book is because you want to be a part of something bigger than yourself.

But it's easy to get caught up in the everyday stuff of life until the years slowly go by, and with each passing year, the question seems to get louder: *Am I making any difference in this world?* Everyone I know wants to have an impact.

One thing I've started to notice is that the way most people measure the difference a person makes is by *how many* and *how much.* How many friends, followers, likes, and comments someone gets on social media determines if they're an *influencer.* How much money and power someone has is how we often gauge a person's impact.

We want to make a difference, but there are so many opinions on the way to do that. We're drowning in content that tells us how to make an impact with our lives. I've read the books, researched the articles, listened to the podcasts, and attended the conferences. I've taken notes as I've studied the autobiographies of difference-makers, trying to understand how they did it. What were their routines? Their habits? Their best practices?

We've never had more access to inspiring and helpful content to help us become people with greater impact and influence, and yet it seems that more people than ever feel like that's not happening in their lives.

Maybe there's another way to make a difference, and we're just missing it.

I wrote this book because I discovered something unexpected when I studied the life of Jesus. Without a doubt, Jesus is the person who has made the biggest difference in all of history, yet his impact is surprising because he didn't follow anything like the formula society gives us. He grew up in a poor family and worked as a carpenter for most of his life. He never traveled far from his small hometown. He never went to college, never was voted into office, never held a title or position that would've stood out on a résumé.

Jesus didn't have thousands of Facebook friends or Instagram followers. He wasn't TikTok famous. He didn't have a YouTube channel. He never tweeted. I'm pretty sure he never even started a podcast.

So, how did Jesus make such a difference in this world? If we study the story of his life as recorded in the Gospels, there are a number of answers we could highlight, but there's one particular phrase that captures how Jesus had such an impact, and I believe it's how he wants to use us to make a difference: *one at a time.*

Before we go on this one at a time journey together, I want you to think back on your life to some of the conversations that influenced you the most. Did they come from a stage or a table? Were they through a podcast or over a cup of coffee? I'm not saying one is wrong and the other is right. And I'm not saying God doesn't use both.

But I am saying that maybe we make changing the world a little more complex than it really is. Maybe we need to stop leaning into the usual ways this world tells us to measure difference-making and start leaning into the unexpected ways God wants to use us.

I don't know what your background is. Maybe you're a businessperson or a stay-at-home parent; maybe you're a pastor, a community leader, or a grandparent; maybe you're a roommate, a classmate, a teammate, a sibling, a neighbor, or a coach. Regardless, I hope as you read this you recognize that wherever God has placed you is a space in which he wants to use you.

Making a difference isn't measured by a viral post or a name on a building. It isn't determined by a following or a fan base. Making a difference isn't dependent on what's in your bank account or who's in your contacts.

Want to make a difference?

Focus on the one. That's it. That's the secret of the way of Jesus. *One at a time.*

PART 1

loving
one
at a time

zoom lens

YOU KNOW HOW SOME MOVIES have a pivotal moment where the whole story changes or a dramatic plot point is revealed? The camera zooms in, and everything else fades into the background because, in that moment, nothing else matters. Let me tell you about one of those moments in my life.

My wife, DesiRae, greeted me at the door when I came home from work. She told me Morgan, our two-year-old, was still napping if I wanted to go wake her up.

I loved that job. I was always excited for the sweet moment.

I walked to Morgan's room, opened the door—and saw the chest of drawers had fallen over and was lying in the middle of the room. It took me a moment before I realized in a panic . . . *my daughter is underneath that dresser!*

Time stopped. Everything else in my life—all of my concerns, my agenda, my goals—blurred out and disappeared. The *only* thing that mattered was Morgan.

In that moment I experienced something I never had before. My father-love turned to panicked terror because my daughter's life was in danger.

I frantically went over and lifted the heavy pine dresser. I threw the drawers off of her. She lay there motionless. I yelled for my wife as I dropped to my knees beside Morgan's still body and examined her. My daughter was breathing but was not conscious. Her entire body was swollen and discolored. Morgan did *not* look like Morgan.

I called 911. That was, in fact, the first time I ever dialed those numbers.

No one answered. It rang and rang and rang. Did I have the wrong number? I hung up and dialed again. No one answered. *Doesn't someone always answer 911 calls?* I yelled into the phone as it kept ringing.

DesiRae held Morgan as we ran out to the car. The two of them got in the back seat and I began to speed out of the neighborhood and head to the hospital.

I opened my phone and tried 911 one more time. It just kept ringing. Morgan needed help, but the people who were supposed to help weren't available. I was furious.

I threw my phone onto the passenger's seat and yelled what I wanted to yell at someone on the other end of the line, "Can someone please help my daughter?!"

The Way of Jesus

I recently googled "most impactful people in history," and it turns out *Time* magazine has ranked them.

Number one? Jesus.

I'm not surprised. Even people who deny that Jesus is Savior or Lord can't deny his influence has swept through history and radically changed the world. You can't even write down today's date without acknowledging that all of history is divided into the time leading up to the birth of Christ and the time since.

When I looked at that list in *Time* that acknowledged no one has had a bigger impact than Jesus, I asked myself, *How did he do it?* I decided to take an afternoon and reread the Gospels with that question in mind. Here's the conclusion I came to:

One at a time.

That's it. That's the secret of the way of Jesus. We are going to see that Jesus did life with a zoom lens. When someone stood in front of him, time stopped. Everything else in his life—all his concerns, his agenda, his plans, his goals—seemed to blur and disappear. The only thing that mattered was the person standing in front of him. Jesus changed the world one person at a time.

After forty-some years of life and twenty-some years of ministry, I've come to the conclusion that Jesus's way of changing the world doesn't come very naturally for me because I'm not great with people. For a long time, I thought that was just the way I was wired, and I chalked it up to my personality. It must just be that Jesus and I didn't share the same Enneagram number.*

People who write books about connecting with people are usually superstars at connecting with people. Me?

*No, Jesus wasn't an Enneagram 1. Being perfect is not the same as being a perfectionist.

That's probably not how you would describe me. I'm not bad at it, but I'm better at sitting in a room by myself, working on my computer by myself, occasionally looking out the window by myself, and getting coffee . . . by myself.*

It's not that I'm a flaming introvert. I usually test on the more extroverted side of the scale. I really do love people and care about connecting with others. I've just never felt like I'm especially good at it. Like Michael Scott as a boss, I'm trying hard but I'm not nearly as impressive as I pretend to be.

Maybe a better analogy is basketball. I love basketball, I'm just no Michael Jordan. And when I say, "I'm no Michael Jordan," I'm not referring to the NBA Hall of Famer; I'm talking about the Michael Jordan who is an American researcher in artificial intelligence.† I feel confident even *that* Michael Jordan is a better basketball player than me.

My point is that we can care about something without necessarily being good at it, and that's how I've often felt when it comes to people. I care about them; I'm just not naturally good with them.

My struggle to connect with people has weighed on me for as long as I can remember. I developed a two-pronged strategy for dealing with my lack of people skills:

1. Avoid it.
2. Fake it.

---

*And wasting time watching Netflix by myself. Not as impressive, but I've read that being vulnerable might help me connect with others.
†Look him up! I wonder how many times he has said the phrase, "Not *that* Michael Jordan."

I'd do my best to avoid social settings where I knew I'd feel awkward trying to connect with people. Not to brag, but I was good at avoiding people whom I thought might make me uncomfortable. For example, if I had to walk through a crowded room, I'd pull out my phone and have an imaginary conversation. With no one else on the line I'd be intensely listening, nodding my head, and doing my best to avoid eye contact with the real people around me.

When people couldn't be avoided, I would fake it, pretending to be a character who's really good at connecting with people. I prepared for social settings by thinking of myself as a charismatic actor‡ who needed to get into character. I had close friends with incredible people skills, and sometimes I'd do my best impression of them.

Unfortunately, that approach felt insincere, mostly because it was. I was pretending to be someone I wasn't. I'm pretty sure that's not what Jesus did. Besides that, faking it is exhausting. Pretending to be a magnetic people person wasn't sustainable. It left me feeling emotionally drained and easily annoyed by people with whom I wanted to connect.

Then it happened. "Then" was 2003. "It" was a new job as a pastor at a huge church. Before working at that church, I had started a new church in Los Angeles County and knew pretty much everybody in it. But I now found myself in a new place with new faces, and I was having a hard time adjusting to *all* the people.

I felt uncomfortable with the huge crowds. *Crowds* isn't a good word for a pastor to use when describing the

‡Dwayne "The Rock" Johnson.

people who come to church. That's a red flag. But that's how I felt. It was a large group of unidentified people. And don't tell them I told you this, but I started to find them to be, well, annoying. I felt irritated by the people I was supposed to love. That's a big problem if you're a pastor.

I knew something was wrong in my heart. I knew God had called me to love and care for his sons and daughters, but I was intentionally not answering the phone. Now, not only was I feeling insecure and anxious about connecting with people, I was also struggling with guilt and shame for feeling that way.

One morning I got to church early and sat in the empty sanctuary and prayed about it. I like to sit in the sanctuary by myself to talk to God and do my devotions. I told God how much I loved people, but I felt like I didn't know *how* to love people.

Crowds to the One

Then, as I sat in that empty sanctuary, I turned to my devotion for that day. It was from Luke 8.

"Now when Jesus returned, a crowd welcomed him, for they were all expecting him" (v. 40). *Ugh. Sorry, Jesus. I know that feeling. A crowd of people with expectations.*

"Then a man named Jairus, a synagogue leader, came and fell at Jesus' feet, pleading with him to come to his house because his only daughter, a girl of about twelve, was dying" (vv. 41–42).

This father desperately needed help for his daughter. I knew that feeling too. No doubt by this point that father had called everyone he could think of, asking for help, but no one was answering his 911 calls. But he still hadn't given up. A good father never does.

As I was reading my devotion and thinking about this father, suddenly it hit me. *The crowds. What happened to the crowds?* I almost forgot about them as I read about this distraught father. The crowds were still there. Jesus was still surrounded by people, but when Jairus stepped in front of Jesus, he became the sole focus of the story, because Jesus's zoom lens was focused only on him.

Jesus agrees to go with Jairus, but then we read, "As Jesus was on his way, the crowds almost crushed him" (v. 42).

There they were again, the crowds. Reading it, I could almost feel my anxiety rising as I thought about crushing crowds. So many people with so many expectations. But then Luke tells us that in the crowd,

> a woman was there who had been subject to bleeding for twelve years, but no one could heal her. She came up behind him and touched the edge of his cloak, and immediately her bleeding stopped.
> "Who touched me?" Jesus asked.
> When they all denied it, Peter said, "Master, the people are crowding and pressing against you." (vv. 43–45)

Mark also tells this story and lets us know the disciples asked Jesus in disbelief, "You see the people crowding against you . . . and yet you can ask, 'Who touched me?'" (Mark 5:31). With such a big crowd, how could he possibly focus in on just one person?

"But Jesus said, 'Someone touched me; I know that power has gone out from me'" (Luke 8:46).

Yes, there was a big crowd, but that's not what Jesus was focused on. The number that mattered to Jesus was the number *one*. It's like taking a picture on your phone of someone standing in a crowd. You put your camera in portrait mode and watch the screen until you spot the person you're looking for, and then zoom in and let the camera focus. In that moment everything else begins to blur and fade into the background. When Jesus was surrounded by the crowds, he had a way of zooming in and focusing on the one.

It's the next verse that changed everything for me. When I read it, I instantly knew it was the secret to Jesus's way of making a difference.

"Then the woman, seeing that she could not go unnoticed . . ." (v. 47).

There was a gigantic group of unidentified people, but she realized Jesus wouldn't let her go unnoticed—not even if she tried. Surrounded by the crushing crowd, she knew the eyes of Jesus wouldn't let her go unseen.

It was like the words came off the page and slapped me in the face. I wasn't just convicted. I was wrecked. God was speaking to me. I realized he called me—he has called each of us who follow Jesus—to make sure that no one goes *unnoticed*.

In a crowd, where is the one who must not go unnoticed? Jesus loves everyone in the crowd, but the way he loves them is one at a time.

In the days to come, I started seeing this on almost every page of the Gospels. Jesus was constantly zooming in on one person at a time.

Jesus goes into Jericho, and people pack the sides of the streets to get a glimpse of him like it's the Macy's Thanksgiving Day Parade, but Jesus focuses on just one person: Zacchaeus (see Luke 19:1–10).

Jesus comes down from a mountain and "large crowds followed him," but a leper shows up, Jesus zooms in, and everyone else is cropped out of the picture (see Matt. 8:1–4).

Jesus goes to a place where a "great number of disabled people used to lie"—there were *lots* of sick people, but we read of "One who was there," and that one gets all of Jesus's attention and is the *only* recipient of a miracle (see John 5:2–9).

Why? Why doesn't Jesus heal all of them? I don't know. But here's what I *do* know: one is the way of Jesus.

I said it before, but I'll say it again, because when it finally hit me, it changed my life. It changed my philosophy of ministry. It changed the legacy I want to leave. I'm hoping it will change yours: Jesus did life with a zoom lens.

When someone stood in front of Jesus, time stopped. Everything else in his life—all his concerns, his agenda, his goals—blurred and disappeared. He was always fully present.

One at a time is the Jesus way of changing the world.

I sat in the sanctuary that morning, and for the first time I prayed a prayer that I have tried to pray every day since: *Jesus, give me your eyes for the one. Help me to see people the way you see people.*

What Do You See?

If you took a course in psychology, you've probably seen the "Spot the Gorilla" video. Six people stand in a circle. Three are in white shirts, three in black. Two hold basketballs. You're asked to watch a one-minute video and keep track of how many times the basketball is passed by the people in white shirts. The six people start moving about and passing the balls. In the middle of the video, a gorilla walks into the crowd of six people, faces the camera, thumps his chest, then steps off screen. The gorilla is in the video for nine seconds.

Would you see the gorilla?

Of course you would. How could a gorilla go unnoticed? Right? Wrong. When they did this experiment at Harvard University, *half* the people didn't see the gorilla. I've ruined the experiment for you to do on yourself, but search for "Spot the Gorilla" on YouTube and try it on someone else.

How could they have missed the gorilla? Simple. It wasn't what they were looking for. They had an agenda: to watch the people in the white shirts and count how many times they passed the basketball. That's how they missed it. They were preoccupied with the crowd and focused on what the crowd was doing.

What do *you* see? In your home? When you're driving? At work? Walking through your neighborhood? At the grocery store?

What do you see? You probably see what you're looking for, what you've trained your eyes to look for. What you've been told to look for. I bet you'd be stunned at what you *don't* see.

At least I was. I began to realize how often I was focusing on the crowds and not noticing the one.

What Did Jesus See?

Forty times in the Gospels we read, "Jesus saw." *Jesus saw* is the launching point of most of the amazing stories of transformed lives. If we want to have the results Jesus had—those amazing stories—we need to do what Jesus did. And doing what Jesus did begins by seeing what Jesus saw.

When I showed up at my new church, I saw the crowds and was bothered by them. But the Bible says, "When [Jesus] saw the crowds, he had compassion on them, because they were harassed and helpless, like sheep without a shepherd" (Matt. 9:36).

I need to be discipled by Jesus. Not just discipled in my relationship with God; I need to be discipled by Jesus in my relationships with people.

When I encountered people, I saw them as those I needed to impress with my imitation people skills. But when Jesus encountered people, he saw God's children.

Remember where we left off in the story? "The woman, seeing that she could not go unnoticed . . ."

Here's what happened next: she "came trembling and fell at his feet. In the presence of all the people, she told why she had touched him and how she had been instantly healed. Then he said to her, 'Daughter, your faith has healed you. Go in peace'" (Luke 8:47–48).

In a society where men didn't talk to women they didn't know, where husbands didn't talk to their wives in public, Jesus spoke to her with a word of affection. But it's the way he referred to her that holds the secret to how he saw her.

He called her *daughter.*

Imagine being this woman. She's been "subject to bleeding" for twelve years. She's spent all her money on alleged cures that never helped. She has nothing. The religious laws of the time stated that her illness made her "unclean." That meant, in addition to dealing with a debilitating sickness, she wasn't allowed to worship at the temple. She was ostracized from her community. She had people tell her, "Your sickness is punishment from God for your sin," and, "If you just had faith, you would be healed."

Worse, if she was married or had kids, she couldn't touch them or touch anything they touched. She had likely been forced to leave them and her home. For twelve years, her life was a living nightmare. Imagine what that was like.

Now imagine she's your daughter.

I had a twelve-minute drive to the hospital filled with panicked terror as I looked in the rearview mirror to see if my daughter was going to make it. Thankfully Morgan went on to make a full recovery, but I'll always remember what it was like to look at my daughter and desperately hope for someone to help her.

How must God have felt watching his daughter suffer the way this woman did for twelve years?

That's what Jesus saw.

Of course he called her daughter.

Seeing with Jesus's Eyes

That morning I read Luke 8, I knew what I had to do.

When I saw the crowds, I had to have "compassion on them" like Jesus did. I began to understand that compassion comes when we see the crowd one person at a time. One daughter, one son at a time.

In the years since, that morning has changed the way I do life. I'll share some of the stories as we journey together through this book. As you read them, remember that this isn't written by someone with an incredibly winsome personality and impressive people skills. But a commitment to one at a time living has changed the way I care for and connect with people.

At the church where I'm a pastor, one at a time has become the way we measure ministry impact. Instead of focusing on how many thousands of people might be in the crowd on a certain Sunday, we're learning to zoom in on one person at a time.

There was a family in our church who had a beautiful five-year-old girl with stage 4 cancer. I prayed for her as she battled her way through round after round of treatments. One day I received a text from her dad: "She's cancer-free! We're having a party to celebrate! You're invited!"

I was thrilled but noticed the party was being held at a church—a *different* church.

I called the dad and said, "Hey, this is so exciting! But why aren't you having the party at our church, at *your* church?"

He explained to me that they'd asked. In fact, they'd tried to reserve a room, but there was a lot of red tape and it seemed like the answer was no. He was incredibly gracious, telling me he understood that we had a large church, that they were just one family among thousands, and we probably had to say no because of all the requests. He was gracious. I, however, was ~~upset~~ furious.

I know our staff in charge of the facilities are awesome servants who love Jesus and love people. They aren't against little girls being healed of cancer, so I tried to understand how this had happened.

One of the staff members explained how much they hated to say no but at some point, in an effort to be fair and equitable, someone had come up with this value: "If we can't do it for everyone, we won't do it for anyone."

The situation started to make more sense to me. We were making decisions based on the crowd rather than the one. And while the value "If we can't do it for everyone, we won't do it for anyone" might work for the government, it doesn't reflect the gospel.

I asked our staff to come up with a value that better reflects the one at a time way of Jesus. Here's what they landed on: "We will do for the one what we wish we could do for everyone."

One More Lesson

For years, trying to connect with people left me feeling frustrated and fatigued, but I started to realize seeing people one at a time was the tool that I'd been missing.

It reminds me of the time I had a belt come off my lawn mower. Well, I think it's called a belt. It's the big, black rubber-band thingy. I could see where it needed to go—around the circular thingy on the mower. I assumed, since the belt was rubbery, I could pull it and stretch it around the circular place it needed to go. I tried. It did not stretch. I tried harder. Nothing. It was time for some Christian cuss words.*

My wife was ~~enjoying~~ watching all of this from the window. She could see my frustration. I was on the edge of a breakdown. I felt like quitting, and she wanted her lawn mowed. I knew what I needed to do, but I just couldn't do it.

My wife came out and said, "Honey, why don't you call the neighbor and ask for help?" But what I heard was, "Since you're not a real man and lack physical strength, why don't you call the neighbor?"

I became more determined to fix the mower myself. I tried and tried—and it sat, broken, in my driveway, for days. It mocked me every time I pulled in. The grass just kept getting taller.

Finally, our kids were getting lost in our jungle, and I knew I had to do something. I called the neighbor. Well, okay, I texted him. It felt less humiliating.

He came over, looked at the mower, and told me what was wrong. *Yeah, I know what's wrong.* He asked, "Do you have a half-inch socket?"

I told him I would be right back. I went into the house and asked my wife, "Um, do you have a half-inch socket? If you do, can I borrow it?"

She went and got it out of her toolbox. She gave it to me, I gave it to my neighbor, and in twenty seconds he had the rubber-band thingy around the circular thingy.

*"Son of a biscuit!"

Wow. I was struggling, but what I really needed was something pretty simple and someone to show me how to use it.

I wanted to love people and make a difference in this world, but I needed help. Jesus gave me a new tool and showed me how to use it.

God had to change me from the inside out, and the essential ingredient he used was praying for others.

We will keep coming back to that in this book, but let's start with a challenge to pray one specific and simple prayer. Praying this prayer every day is where we begin our one at a time adventure.

Jesus, give me your eyes for the one. Help me to see people the way you see people.

in then *through*

WHAT IS THE MOST that one person you don't know has ever mattered to you?

Read that again.

What is the most that one person *you don't know* has ever mattered to you?

I'm not asking how much someone you know matters to you. I'm asking about someone you don't know. That may be hard to answer. You may wonder, *Isn't that like asking, "What's your favorite meal that you've never eaten?" or "Where's your favorite place to visit that you've never gone?"*

How can someone matter to you if you don't know them?

I Need to Do Something

In 2010 my family spent a month in the Dominican Republic to do mission work with some friends who serve there. The second day we were there, I was sleeping in a bunk bed and was awakened by shaking. Immediately, I knew it was an earthquake, but I didn't know how far away the epicenter was or how devastating it would be. I soon learned a massive earthquake had struck Haiti, on the other side of the island.

You may remember seeing the catastrophic images on the news: 7.0 magnitude, two hundred and fifty thousand lives lost, more than three hundred thousand people injured, and five million people displaced. I didn't know it when I sat up in that bed, but in that moment tens of thousands of children became orphans.

That earthquake radically changed the plans our family had for how we would spend the next month. For more than a year, we'd been preparing for this mission trip to the Dominican Republic. All those plans quickly changed, and I found myself on a tiny plane filled with emergency supplies, crossing over the mountains and landing on a tiny airstrip in a small Haitian town called Jacmel.

It's hard to describe how different the devastation feels when you're actually there. A few minutes after we had left the airport, I noticed an overwhelming stench in the air. I asked the Haitian pastor I was with what I was smelling. He answered me with one word: "Death."

Building after building had collapsed. Rubble was everywhere.

People were everywhere. Crowds of people walked around in stunned disbelief, wailing, shouting out names of loved ones they couldn't find, combing through the debris. Some were searching for something, but most were searching for *someone*. I walked through the streets, numb, looking around at this gigantic group of desperate human suffering, and then I saw her.

Zoom lens.

Everything else blurred out and disappeared.

She was probably two years old, sitting all by herself, no one in her immediate area. I walked over to check on her. She saw me coming and looked up. Tears filled her eyes. She lifted her arms for me to pick her up and hold her. I scooped her up and held her, but I didn't know what to do. I was hit by a wave of those same helpless, powerless feelings I'd had when I'd moved that dresser and lifted my unconscious two-year-old daughter off the floor.

I wasn't watching crowds of random people on the news from the comfort of my home. I couldn't change the channel. It's one thing to read about hundreds of thousands of people who have been impacted; it's another to hold one in your arms.

I need to do something. I looked for her parents. I asked around, but no one seemed to know where they were.

I need to do something. There were people in makeshift tents along the side of the road. I took the girl over to them, but they were preoccupied with their own problems.

I need to do something. Finally, I found a girl who was maybe nine years old who seemed to know the little one I was carrying and was willing to take care of her. I left her there. I don't know if that was the right thing to do.

The Power of One

I didn't know that little girl. I didn't even know her name, but she mattered to me, and even though I tried, I couldn't forget about her. When we got back to Kentucky, we continued to send financial support, but I mostly tried to move on from what I had experienced in Haiti. A few months later I was looking through a stack of pictures someone had taken while we were in Haiti and saw there was one of me holding that little girl. I tried not to look at it.

Somehow that picture started showing up on my screen saver rotation. Whenever my computer would start cycling through images, she would come up.

Even though I was no longer there or holding her in my arms, I still couldn't shake the thought. *I need to do something.*

That's the power of one.

Most of us regularly have those *I need to do something* moments. We feel compelled to make a difference—but how?

After enough moments of feeling like we should do something but not knowing what to do, we learn to silence that voice. *I need to do something* gets replaced with *Somebody should do something.* It's not that we don't *want* to do something, it's just that we don't know *what* to do.

For a long time when I felt compelled to do something, I would pray, *God, what do you want to do through me?*

What I have learned along the way is that often my first prayer should be, *God, what do you want to do* in *me?*

Because the work God does *in* you will lead to the work God wants to do *through* you. This radically changes our approach to being difference-makers. As much as I might want to skip the *in* and go straight to the *through*, God's approach is consistently in *then* through.

Time Alone with God

In Mark 1, Jesus was surrounded by people in need. Verse 33 says that "the whole town gathered at the door" where Jesus was staying. Everyone needed him to do something for them. Jesus always seemed to know what to do. He always seemed to understand how to make a difference in someone's life.

How did Jesus always know what to do? A number of times throughout the Gospels, Jesus made it clear that he didn't say or do anything except what he was directed to by his Father.* Even Jesus modeled an "in then through" approach to making a difference.

After the entire town gathered outside his door, Jesus had another full day of ministry scheduled, but we read in verse 35, "Very early in the morning, while it was still dark, Jesus got up, left the house, and went off to a solitary place, where he prayed."

He got away from the crowds and went to a place where no one would see him to spend time with his heavenly Father. When the disciples woke up, people were already at the door, needing something from Jesus. They went to look for him, "and when they found him, they exclaimed: 'Everyone is looking for you!'" (v. 37). There were all kinds of people with all kinds of needs and expectations, but Jesus knew *what* to do. He replied

*See John 5:18–19; 8:28; and 12:49.

to the disciples, "'Let us go somewhere else—to the nearby villages—so I can preach there also. That is why I have come.' So he traveled throughout Galilee, preaching in their synagogues and driving out demons" (vv. 38–39).

Jesus spent time alone with God and was reminded of why he had come. He was refocused on his purpose. He knew what God wanted to do *through* him because he started the day by giving attention to God's work *in* him.

Noticing the Dust

Mother Teresa spent most of her life ministering to the poor and suffering in the slums of Calcutta. I've heard dozens of Mother Teresa stories over the years, and she seemed to always see the person in need and know what to do to meet that need.

I recently read a story in which Mother Teresa was in Australia and came across an elderly Aborigine man who lived in absolute squalor. Mother Teresa wrote, "I can assure you that you have never seen a situation as difficult as that poor old man's."[1]

I imagine myself in that situation, and I'm pretty sure I would feel incapable of helping. But Mother Teresa? She told the man she was going to clean his house, wash his clothes, and make his bed. He said no, but her insistence overcame his refusal.

While cleaning the house, Mother Teresa discovered a lamp covered with dust. She asked the man, "Don't you light your lamp? Don't you ever use it?"

He answered, "No. No one comes to see me. I have no need to light it. Who would I light it for?"

She asked him if he would light it if the local nuns came to visit. He replied, "Of course." That day the local nuns committed to visiting him every evening. Two years later, Mother Teresa said she had completely forgotten that man until she received a message from him: "Tell my friend that the light she lit in my life continues to shine still."

It's an amazing story. I'm afraid if I met that man, cleaning his house and making his bed wouldn't occur to me. If I saw a dusty old lamp, I wouldn't ask, "Don't you light your lamp?" I would think, *Hmm, that sure is a dusty lamp.*

I get that using Mother Teresa as an example to follow of loving people one at a time seems a little out of reach. But what strikes me about that story and many others I've read about her is the fact that the "something" she did was usually something I could do. She didn't write this man a huge check or perform a complicated surgery. She made his bed and washed his clothes.

But still, Mother Teresa was a nun who lived in the slums on the other side of the globe. So let me tell you about Linda Wilson-Allen.

Linda was featured in a front-page article in the *San Francisco Chronicle.*[2] Linda is no nun; she's a metro bus driver. Why the article? The big news about Linda is that she *loves* the people who ride on her bus.

A reporter for the *Chronicle* took that bus, and he couldn't understand what was happening on it. Linda, the driver, knew all the regulars. She learned their names. She waited for them if they were not at the stop when she got there.

One day the reporter watched Linda get out of the bus to help an elderly woman struggling with heavy grocery bags. Another day Linda discovered that a woman in the bus shelter was new to town. She invited her to come over for Thanksgiving. There is story after story of Linda Wilson-Allen connecting with and serving the people who rode her bus. She was always doing *something*.

The stories don't seem especially noteworthy, but they became newsworthy! I'm afraid if I drove a metro bus, I'd show up on time, drive carefully, and secretly wear headphones so I could listen to podcasts and if necessary take imaginary phone calls.

I'd mostly avoid eye contact and at the most give out an occasional head nod. It's not that I wouldn't want to do something, it's that I wouldn't know what to do, and the something I could come up with would seem too ordinary.

But one at a time begins when you

1. See someone.
2. Do something.

The Secret Sauce

That sounds simple, but it isn't easy. At least it's not easy for me. What I've learned is that *seeing someone* and *doing something* requires an in then through approach.

I read an interview with Mother Teresa in which she was asked what she did in the morning. She answered, "Pray."

The journalist asked, "When do you start?"

Mother Teresa said, "Half past four."

The interviewer next asked what Mother Teresa did *after* she prayed. She said, "We try to pray through our work by doing it with Jesus, for Jesus, to Jesus."

So, in case you missed that: after she prayed, she kept praying.

Mother Teresa was also asked what special qualities allowed her to make such a massive impact. Her response: "I don't claim anything of the work. It is His work. I am like a little pencil in His hand, that is all. He does the thinking. He does the writing. The pencil has nothing to do with it. The pencil has only to be allowed to be used."[3]

In the *San Francisco Chronicle* article, the mystified reporter asked Linda Wilson-Allen how she was able to have a loving attitude and take such servant-hearted actions toward those who rode her bus. What he learned? "Her mood is set at 2:30 a.m. when she gets down on her knees to pray for 30 minutes."[4]

John Ortberg, a pastor in the San Francisco area, interviewed Linda at his church. He asked about her 2:30 prayer time. She said, "So we talk. I ask God to show me my life, so he shows me my life. He puts things in front of us. He could be working on my patience, or it could be someone less fortunate than I am, to give them some shoes, or whatever the case may be. He'll show you. That's where my kindness comes from."[5]

John asked if she also prayed while she was on the job, driving the bus. She replied, "Yes, when I'm out there doing my job ministering. I call it ministering. So, you see things. God will show you things. He will show you the senior who's having a hard time getting up on that coach, and how to take it in real gentle and set it down right in front of her. He'll teach you the one who's in the back who might not have all their fare, and he'll say, 'Maybe they just pay what they can.' He'll teach you these things. He just shows you."[6]

She didn't call it *driving*; she called it *ministering*. She started with prayer and then she kept praying.

Whenever that picture of the two-year-old girl in Haiti would pop up as a screen saver, I'd think to myself, *I need to do something.* But I didn't know what to do.

So I started to pray. I prayed for her and for the other children in Haiti. I wanted God to do something *through* me to make a difference, but I realized I first needed to pray about what he wanted to do *in* me.

In Then Through

We live in a "there's an app for that" culture. Our values of convenience and efficiency have led to the popularity of "life hacks"—finding a more expedient way to get something done. You can clean your keyboard with the adhesive side of a sticky note, use dental floss to make perfectly shaped cinnamon rolls, put tea bags in your smelly shoes to take away the funky foot odor, or use a straw to easily remove the stem of a strawberry.

In a sermon, I mentioned a grilled cheese "food hack" I'd read about where you lay a toaster on its side and put in your bread and cheese. A minute later you have a perfect grilled cheese sandwich without the hassle of a frying pan and spatula and having to flip it in the middle of cooking. It sounded ideal. Except that some people actually took my advice and tried it—and reported that this food hack was more like a fire hazard that filled their kitchens with smoke.

"Life hacks" and "food hacks" are popular because we're always trying to find a way to make life easier and be more productive with less work. We want increased output with decreased input. That's especially true when it comes to making a difference in someone's life. I think we'd love a "spiritual impact hack." In fact, that may be why we pick up books like this one. We want God to use us in significant ways, we want the amazing stories, we want to leave a legacy, and we want it *now*.

I'm sorry to tell you that there's no hack for connecting with people, loving them like Jesus did, and having real spiritual influence. The "spiritual impact hack" that we most often attempt is to pray, "God, do something through me."

There is, of course, nothing wrong with asking God to do something through you that would have an impact on people and make a difference in this world. That's a great prayer. The problem is that we want God to do something *through* us without inviting him to do something *in* us first.

We have a hard time making the connection between getting up very early in the morning while it's still dark to pray and making a difference with our lives during the day. We focus on what we want God to do through us, but impact almost always follows the formula of in *then* through.

The Way of the Seed

In Matthew 13, Jesus told a parable about a farmer who threw some seeds. Different seeds fell on different types of soil. Some fell on soil that was too hard or too shallow, so the seeds didn't sink in and take root. Other seeds fell on good soil, took root, grew, and eventually produced a harvest.

Jesus used an agricultural metaphor because there were many farmers in his audience that day, but also because a seed is a great example of the in then through way that God works. God created seeds to create a harvest. He hardwired the harvest into the seed. He designed it so the right conditions and right soil would bear fruit.

Sometimes people read this parable and think of themselves as the farmer. The farmer is the hero of the story. The farmer is making things happen. The farmer is doing something. But to be clear, in this parable *Jesus* is the farmer and we are the soil. He's the farmer who wants to bring a harvest through us, but he first must do his work *in* us.

Our focus tends to be on the harvest, but first we need to give our attention to the condition of the soil. Farmers want a bountiful harvest, but they know it won't happen unless they take care of the soil. The fruit they want to come out of the ground won't happen unless the right things first happen in the ground.

Think of what God does through you as the harvest that comes up out of the ground. It's the fruit that starts to grow. That's what we tend to give our attention to, because that's what we can see and what other people notice. That's what gets us attention and likes. We can't see what's happening in the ground, so it's easy to overlook and underestimate.

Besides, it's a lot of work. We would all love to be on the front page of the paper, but who wants to wake up at

2:30 in the morning to pray for the people we will come into contact with during the day?

Dirty Work

There are a number of farms close to my home that will let you pay to harvest what's growing in their fields. They hand you a basket, and you can go pick your own apples or strawberries. However, it's actually just as cheap, if not cheaper, to buy those apples or strawberries at the grocery store. The farm is charging you to do the work of harvesting, and people pay for it because harvesting is enjoyable.

But imagine a scenario where the farm charged people to come during planting season and till the ground and cultivate the soil with the promise that when the harvest comes, you'll get a basket of the fruit. *Nobody* is going to pay money for the opportunity to spend the day preparing the soil for seed. The harvest is fun and the reward is immediate, but what's happening in the ground is hard work.

When I give my attention to what God wants to do in me, I've discovered he will always do something through me. Philippians 2:13 says, "It is God who works in you," but why? The verse continues: ". . . to will and to act in order to fulfill his good purpose."

Seed Work

It's not just Mother Teresa and Linda Wilson-Allen; throughout Scripture we consistently see the in then through way God uses people.

God wants to work through Moses to rescue his people. But God first works in Moses for *forty years* as he works in obscurity for his father-in-law on the back side of the desert.

God gives Joseph a dream about what God's going to do through him, but there is some soil work that needs to take place first. Joseph spends a significant amount of time as a slave and then in prison. It may have seemed the dream was dead and God had forgotten about him—but no, God was doing something in him.

David is anointed king, and God is going to do powerful things through him, but first David spends several decades on the run because his life is threatened by King Saul. As David hides out in different caves, God is doing something in him. In Psalm 139, David prays for God to be at work in him:

> Search me, O God, and know my heart;
>   test me and know my anxious thoughts.
> Point out anything in me that offends you,
>   and lead me along the path of everlasting life.
> (vv. 23–24 NLT)

Pray God would do great things *through* you, but first ask him to do his work *in* you.

If farming brought an instant harvest, I think it'd be a more popular occupation. Recently I was cleaning out a junk drawer in our house when I found some seed packets. A sweet elderly lady at church had given them to me for Christmas. There were watermelon seeds and pumpkin seeds, and I thought, *That's great! We eat watermelons and like pumpkin pie.*

That was years ago. We never did anything with those seeds. And that day I just stuck them back in the drawer. (Apparently, that isn't an especially conducive environment for plant growth to take place.)

I had seeds and the potential for harvest, but they had to be planted in soil and cultivated. From time to time, I would be hungry for watermelon and remember the seeds in the junk drawer. The problem was I wanted an immediate harvest, and that's not how it works. First some work had to take place in the ground.

I Need to Do Something

I didn't know that little girl in Haiti, but for nearly three years the picture of me holding her would pop up on my computer. I'd feel the same Molotov cocktail of emotions I'd had in that moment—compassion, desperation, powerlessness, helplessness. Every time I was also overcome by the same thought I had then: *I need to do something.*

Over those three years, I kept praying, "God, do something through me," but it turns out God had some work he needed to do *in* me. He was helping me learn to live like a pencil in his hand.

Then something started to grow out of the ground. One day I was in our prayer room at church, where there are hundreds of prayer requests posted on the wall. I was praying for some of the requests when I came across one that read, "Pray for our friends who are raising money and finalizing their adoption of a five-year-old girl from Haiti."

That was about how old the girl I'd held that day would've been.

Most of these prayer requests don't have names on them. This one did. Now, you aren't supposed to take prayer requests out of the room. You're supposed to leave them so other people can pray too. But I stole that prayer request. I took it home and showed it to my wife. We prayed together and agreed that we wanted to reach out to that couple and help cover whatever adoption expenses they had left.

I was thankful to finally have the opportunity to do *something*. I thought that was God answering my prayer and it would be the end of the story, but the picture kept popping up on my screen.

I picked up my phone and texted Toby, a friend of mine who attended our church in Louisville whom I knew had a heart for the people of Haiti. I asked, "Hey, can we grab coffee? I feel like I need to share with you something God has put on my heart. I'm not sure what to do with it, but maybe we could chat?"

What I didn't know, when we sat down at a Starbucks a week later, was that Toby had been making regular trips to Haiti. Want to guess where he was flying? A tiny airstrip in a small Haitian town named Jacmel.

I started telling Toby about what happened with the little girl. I opened my computer and showed him the picture. I explained I'd been praying for three years and felt like I had to do something, and I wondered if maybe that something was helping to start an orphanage.

A huge smile came over Toby's face, and I asked, "What's so funny?"

Over that coffee, back in 2013, Toby told me all about the orphans he had been helping care for and their need for a school. We started making trips together. In 2014 our families spent several months in Jacmel and worked with local Haitian pastors to help establish an orphanage and start a school.

Last time I visited, I spent time with dozens and dozens of kids from that small town who were around the age of the little girl I'd held after the earthquake. I've often wondered if she was one of the girls growing up in the orphanage or attending the school.

Do Something in Me

I know you and I may be frustrated. We keep praying God would do something *through* us, because we want to make a difference with our lives but it doesn't seem like much is happening. We want to impact a classmate or a coworker. We're trying to do some things differently in our marriage and as a parent, but our spouse and kids don't seem to notice. It doesn't feel like the seed is planted; it feels like the seed is *buried*. Nothing seems to be happening.

We know we need to do something, and we keep praying that God would show us what to do, but what if we first prayed a different prayer?

Instead of praying *God, do something* through *me*, pray, *God, do something* in *me*.

Then see what happens.

Will you try something this week? You don't have to wake up very early in the morning while it's still dark, but set your alarm fifteen minutes earlier than you normally would and take that time to pray through your day.

Pray that God would give you ears to listen to him. Pray that he would give you his eyes for the people around you. Ask him to search your heart and point out anything that needs attention. Pray that what he wants you to say and do will overflow out of what he's doing in your heart.

And then trust that something is happening in the soil that will soon break through the ground.

the proximity
principle

ON A HOT SOUTHERN CALIFORNIA DAY, I sat on the curb of a street just down from Skid Row and listened to a "one at a time" story about a sweet elderly lady from the Midwest who got lost in South Central LA.

She was wandering down a back alley that was notorious for gang activity. She'd come to LA on a mission trip with people from her church but somehow got separated from her group. She had no idea where she was or how to get where she needed to be. Then she saw him.

He grew up in a street gang, had worked as a hired gun, and had spent the last several years in prison. In fact, he'd been released from prison that very day.

What do you do if you're that old lady, lost in South Central LA with a scary-looking dude covered in gang tattoos coming at you?

I know what I'd do: turn around and run.* It'd also be a good time for her to have a loud imaginary phone conversation with her pretend grandson, the FBI agent.

Collecting Maps

I recently read a blog post about a book called *The Island of the Lost Maps*, written by Miles Harvey, which tells the mostly true story of a map thief named Gilbert Bland. Bland would steal old and precious maps from libraries across America and then sell them. Harvey talked about why he was drawn to a story about a thief who stole and sold old maps.

In my 30s I spent a great deal of time at a travelers' café in Chicago whose walls were adorned with maps from Bali and whose shelves were filled with maps and guides to far-flung destinations. I was then the literary critic for *Outside Magazine*, a great job but one that was beginning to wear on my patience. You see, the books I read were about people who climbed Himalayan peaks, rode a bicycle all the way across Africa, sailed wooden boats across the Atlantic, or tracked into restricted areas of China. These tales of adventure filled my days and my imagination, and yet my own life was anything but adventurous. The interior of the coffee shop was ringed by clocks, each one showing the time in some distant locale, and as I watched the weeks ticking away in these distant places, I began to long for an adventure of my own.[1]

*Or in her case, speed walk like she's at the mall before the stores open.

Harvey also said that he reminded himself of a character in a Joseph Conrad novel who would look at maps and say, "When I grow up, I will go there."

Most of us understand that approach to life. We look at maps that promise adventure and we think to ourselves, *Someday. Someday I will go there. It's not practical now—but someday. I'm overwhelmed with responsibilities right now—but someday. When I'm a little more prepared. When I have a little more time. When I have better directions. When it's a little safer. Someday I will go there.*

And so we sit and stare at clocks and watch the weeks go by. We look at pictures someone else has taken. We read stories someone else has written. We watch television shows about the life someone else is living. And we don't seem to be aware of the irony. We spend our days staring at maps—but we never go on an adventure.

I feel that way sometimes when I study the one at a time stories in Scripture or the biographies of missionaries. When I read those stories, something comes alive in me, but most of the time I don't go anywhere.

Can you imagine how it'll feel to look back at your life and realize there were adventures God intended for you to have, but you never experienced them? There was a purpose God made you for, but you never lived it? There were opportunities God put in front of you, but you never took them? There were stories you were meant to be a part of, but you turned and ran in the opposite direction?

I desperately don't want that for me, or for you, so we definitely need to figure out what it looks like to live out the adventure of God's will for our lives. The good news is when God sent his Son to earth, he also sent us a map.

God's Will Is . . .

On the night Jesus was arrested to be crucified, he spent some time with his closest followers and talked about his will. John 13 records some of his final words to them. After explaining he wouldn't be with them much longer, he reminded them of one of his primary purposes for them. In verse 34, Jesus said, "A new command I give you: Love one another."

It's not a new suggestion, idea, proposition, or recommendation but a new *command*. But why does Jesus call it "new"? It's not new. Loving others was often his central message. What Jesus said next is what made it new: "As I have loved you, so you must love one another" (v. 34).

Jesus had shown them a new way to love. In fact, the disciples heard these words with freshly washed feet. Moments earlier Jesus had knelt down and humbly washed the dust and dirt and grime out from between their toes.

They knew what he meant when he told them his will was for them to love others the way he had loved them. It's a love that puts others' needs ahead of our own. It's the kind of love that considers others better than ourselves. It's the kind of love that doesn't insist on its own way or keep a record of wrongs.

One of the words that best captures the love of Jesus is *proximity*. At Christmas, we celebrate that Jesus loves us enough to come be with us. That's what *Emmanuel* means: "God *with* us." The incarnation of Christ, Jesus coming to earth, makes it clear that the way he loves requires proximity. It's hard to love someone if you're determined to keep your distance.

Power of Proximity

I have no sense of direction.

My wife has an ~~uncanny~~ annoying sense of direction.

Don't misunderstand me. My wife is amazing; it's her perfect sense of direction that's annoying. No matter where she is, she knows which way is north, south, east, and west. I can never remember where I parked my car, but she knows the longitude and latitude. Wherever she is, she always knows the right way to go.

She has a perfect sense of direction, but she doesn't like to drive. That means I'm in charge of the driving and she's in charge of the navigating. That tends to go about as well as you might expect. I sometimes wonder if God decided for us to do a lifetime of traveling together for his own amusement. Sometimes when we're arguing in the car, I want to look up toward heaven and shout, "Are you not entertained?"

My directional instincts never seem to be right. What feels like the right direction rarely takes me to where I want to end up.

If I'm honest, my instinct doesn't usually lead me toward opportunities to love people either. Left to my own devices, I won't go to the places and people God wants me to love. In fact, my natural impulse is usually to turn around and go the opposite direction.

My instinct isn't proximity; my instinct is *distance*, especially when it comes to four categories of people that we will talk about a lot in this book:

1. Difficult people.
2. Draining people.

3. Different people.
4. *Dungeons and Dragons* players.*

But I've learned that if I'm following Jesus and loving people the way he did, it'll mean constantly being pointed in a direction that doesn't feel natural or comfortable.

Going Far to Get Close

Did you hear the one about Jesus and the naked, bloody guy who lived in a graveyard? As you might guess, he was the kind of guy most of us would try to avoid. We read about him in Mark 5. We'll get there, but first we need to read Mark 4 for context. Jesus was teaching and "a very large crowd soon gathered around him" (v. 1 NLT).

Crowds, always crowds.

Jesus spent most of the day teaching all these people. But "that day when evening came, he said to his disciples, 'Let us go over to the other side'" (v. 35).

Jesus turned to his twelve bros and told them to hop in the boat because they needed to go across the lake. That was surprising, because the "other side" was the Gerasene region, which was an area people normally tried to avoid. No doubt the disciples didn't want to go, but Jesus was the one giving directions. "So they took Jesus in the boat and started out, leaving the crowds behind" (v. 36 NLT).

The disciples didn't know it yet, but Jesus was leaving behind the crowds and moving toward the one. It was

*Just kidding! (But not really.)

nighttime, they were in the boat going across the lake—
and chaos erupted. A huge storm came up, sending waves
breaking across the boat. Jesus's guys, several of whom
were professional fishermen, were terrified, and they were
screaming, "We're going to drown!"

The only course of action that made sense was to turn
around, but they didn't. Apparently, Jesus *had to* go to the
region of the Gerasenes.

Finally, they arrived. They stayed for only a very short
part of that day—maybe a couple hours. Only *one thing*
happened during that time. Then they went straight back.

On their way back, the disciples must have thought,
*Man, we nearly lost our lives to get there. Jesus was willing
to risk everything for that one thing.*

So, what was that one thing?

A man. *One* man.

This guy's life was in complete turmoil. It was so bad,
and he was considered so dangerous, that he was kept
locked up in a cemetery far away from town. He never
wore clothes and would cut his body with jagged rocks he
found in the graveyard.†

Everyone considered him a monster. But if you looked
at him through Jesus's zoom lens, you wouldn't have seen
a monster, you would've seen a man in misery. No one
would get close to him; in fact, they went out of their way
to avoid him.

One of the ways you know Jesus is directing your life is
you find yourself in the close proximity of one person at a

†One of my friends preached a sermon about this guy and called it "A
Nude Dude in a Rude Mood." I felt like you should know that.

time—one difficult, one draining, one different person at a time.

Risky Proximity

Too often what stops us is fear.

One of my favorite places to speak is at church services in prisons. That hasn't always been true. For a long time, I avoided places like that, but Jesus kept pointing me in that direction. I tried to just send books and video series, but Jesus wanted there to be proximity.

A few years ago, I was speaking to a group of inmates at a local state prison. I'll never forget one man who came up to share his story with me. I had noticed this man worshiping earlier in the evening, and he captured my attention. We were very different. He was a big man who had clearly spent some time in the gym. He had tattoos that ran up both arms and crept up his neck too.

When he walked up to me, he pulled a photograph out of his Bible. It was a picture of him as a younger man standing in a driveway. The picture was taken from the house, so you could see the street behind him. He handed me the picture and said, "I lived at this place for seven years. Take a look at this and tell me what you notice about this picture."

I took a few minutes to study it. It looked like it was taken on a summer day. His shirt had the sleeves cut off, and you could see his tattoos. He had a grease rag sticking out of his front pocket and was holding a beer up to the camera with one hand. I wasn't sure what I was looking for. I kept looking. I could see he was getting emotional, and I desperately wanted to notice what my brother wanted me to see.

And then I saw it in the background. It was across the street and a little out of focus. I handed the picture back to him and said, "You lived across the street from a church."

And then without really thinking about it, I instinctively said, "I'm sorry."

I knew where this conversation was going.

It wasn't my church. I wasn't its pastor. I'd never set foot inside those doors. But I was sorry because I knew what the story was going to be. Sure enough, he had lived there for seven years and not one time did someone from the church come over to his house and knock on his door. Not one time did its pastor introduce himself.

There were some Sunday mornings he would be in his driveway working on his motorcycle, and he'd watch as people came into this small neighborhood church in their Sunday suits and dresses. It's not that they didn't see him, but they were careful not to look at him or make eye contact. The only interaction he had with the church was an occasional note in his mailbox letting him know that his grass was too long and it needed to get mowed.

After he told me his story, he asked me, "Why didn't someone at least cross the street and tell me about Jesus? Maybe I wouldn't have come, but why didn't someone at least invite me to come to church? I don't understand. Why didn't even one person walk across the street after church and just talk to me?"

He could only imagine how differently things would've gone if he would have become a follower of Jesus at that time in his life. But in a drunken rage he'd killed another man, so he's now spending decades in prison, where he carries around a Bible with a photograph of him in his front yard with a church across the street. He was so close. It was right there. He woke up every morning, stepped out his front door, and stood in the shadow of the cross that sat on top of the building. People walked in and out of it carrying Bibles like the one that changed his life.

He wanted to know, "Why didn't someone just walk across the street?"

At first I assumed his question was rhetorical, because the answer to me, as someone who grew up in the church, seemed so obvious. But he stared at me in silence, and I realized he didn't know. I told him the truth. "You were so different from them and they were afraid."

As I explained this to him, I think he suspected as much but just didn't want to believe it. He was angry but mostly sad, and he said, "That's not okay."

He was right, of course, but I wasn't surprised by what that church had failed to do—not because I knew the church or the pastor. I wasn't surprised because I know me, and I'm not sure I would've made it across the street either.

There's something in us that wants to follow Jesus but doesn't want to cross the street. We want to do God's will as long as the map doesn't lead us out of our comfort zones.

Following Jesus to the One

The book of Acts tells the stories of the first Jesus-followers.

In chapter 8 we read about one follower named Philip who demonstrated the priority of proximity. He was in

Samaria working with a new church. Philip was leading a *revival*.

> But now the people believed Philip's message of Good News concerning the Kingdom of God and the name of Jesus Christ. As a result, many men and women were baptized. (Acts 8:12 NLT)

Did you notice it said "many"? Philip was being used by God in a *big* way to impact lots of people. Then, in the midst of this, "an angel of the Lord said to [Philip], 'Go south down the desert road that runs from Jerusalem to Gaza.' So he started out" (vv. 26–27 NLT).

Why would God send Philip, one of the most significant leaders of the early church, away from where hundreds of lives were being impacted, to this desert road?

Because of a man. *One* man.

It's incredible the lengths God will go to reach one person. There were crowds in Samaria, but one at a time is the Jesus way of changing the world.

I love that the angel told Philip to leave his successful ministry to go down a road, without any explanation as to why, and the next verse begins, "So he started out." Philip didn't know why he was being asked to go, but he went. He didn't object to the direction. He didn't even ask questions.

If *you and I* want to experience God's will for our lives, we need to listen for and be obedient to God's voice. If we follow, we'll walk into an amazing story God is writing and wants us to be a part of.

Philip didn't know why he was being told to go, but "he started out, and he met the treasurer of Ethiopia, a eunuch of great authority" (v. 27).

If you're a dude and know what "eunuch" means, that word probably caused you to pause. If you don't know, you might want to sit down for this: a eunuch is a man who's had his private parts removed. It was done back then to guys who worked in the palace to make sure they weren't messing around with the girls in the palace. It was a job requirement.* That's why the Ethiopian eunuch was a eunuch.

Because he was an Ethiopian, and especially because he was a eunuch, people back then would have looked at him like God was *not* for him. He was *different*. But . . . *Jesus, help me see people the way you see people.*

When Philip met him, the eunuch was sitting in his chariot reading the book of Isaiah from the Old Testament. Having a chariot back then would be like owning a Rolls Royce today. He had a lot, but he was still searching for more. I wonder if God has put people in your life who have a lot, so you assume they wouldn't be interested in hearing about Jesus, but what you don't know is that they're searching for more.

This Ethiopian man was seeking, and "the Spirit told Philip, 'Go to that chariot and stay near it'" (v. 29).

Just like Philip, if we follow God's leading, we're going to end up chasing some chariots. There's no way this guy could be influenced by Philip *unless* Philip was in close proximity to him.

*I used to think wearing a tie to work was a lot to ask.

The chariot you chase might be the gym where you work out. The grocery store you shop at. The café or restaurant where you're a regular. I think for sure it's your workplace and the neighborhood you live in.

God's going to put you in close proximity to people who are far from him and give you divine appointments to share Jesus with them. To show up for them, you won't be able to stay where you are.

That's what happened with Philip. Think about it: A man from Ethiopia, who spoke a different language but somewhere along the line must have learned Greek, traveled a thousand miles by chariot and was on a desert road reading the Bible—and along came Philip. This was not a random accident; it was a God-given appointment.

What if you stopped assuming people in your proximity are there by random accident? The person next to you on the plane, the server at your table in the restaurant, the stylist or barber cutting your hair, the parent or grandparent who sits next to you at your kid's game, the family who lives next door—what if you started considering them divine appointments God has known about since the beginning of time and has carefully orchestrated so your paths would cross at just the right moment?

Philip "ran up to the chariot" and got to share Jesus (v. 30). I *love* how Philip did it. As we journey together through this book, we're going to learn from Jesus how to have a conversation about Jesus, and Philip did it perfectly.

He started with a question, drawn from their immediate situation.

He listened.

He shared the "good news about Jesus" (v. 35). What we have to share with people is *good* news about *Jesus*. Philip didn't share his morals or his values or his political views. He pointed to Jesus and got personal enough to invite the Ethiopian man to take a next step closer to God.

And the result?

> As they traveled along the road, they came to some water and the eunuch said, "Look, here is water. What can stand in the way of my being baptized?" And he gave orders to stop the chariot. Then both Philip and the eunuch went down into the water and Philip baptized him. (vv. 36–38)

Wow. What a story! And *God has stories like that planned for you.* But to step into those stories, you can't stay where you are. You are going to have to get out of the house. There will be times when your gut tells you to run away, but Jesus tells you to run *toward*.

Stare at the Potential Reward

To do what God wants requires proximity, and proximity is risky. It was risky for Jesus to go into a graveyard to talk to a naked, bloody lunatic. It was risky for Philip to leave the revival and walk down that desert road.

It'll feel risky for you to talk to your coworker about your faith, or start a spiritual conversation with your server, or invite your neighbor to church. We need to overcome the fear and take the risk.

Do you know the key to staring down fear? It's staring at the potential return.

Your willingness to risk is *always* based on the potential reward.

For instance, you wouldn't run into a burning house. Why? It's a risk, and your fear of taking that risk would be too great. But you *would* run into a burning house if your child was inside it. Why? It's the same risk and would induce the same fear, but you'd do it because the potential return—saving your child—is worth it.

Too often we avoid getting close to someone far from God and stay away from draining, difficult, and different people because there is risk. We might be rejected. We could look stupid. We may not be able to answer their questions.

When we stare at the risk, we are stopped by our fear. But we can stare down the risk by staring at the potential return.

Each person we find ourselves in close proximity with is a child of God. God's will is for you to love that person the way Jesus has loved you.

We are scared of risk, but I think what we need to be scared of is regret.

We don't want to get to the end of our lives and realize we missed the purpose, the adventures, and the stories God planned for us.

Cross the Alley

Remember that alley in South Central LA? What do you do if you're an elderly lady and a scary, just-released-from-prison gang guy is walking toward you?

That gang guy is a friend of mine named Alfred Lomas.[2] Alfred spent twenty-nine years in a gang. Since age twelve, his life had been violence and drugs. As we sat on a curb he told me that he was the one on the other side of the alley that day. He laughed as he told me how that elderly woman headed toward him. He was confused. She said hello and asked if he was hungry. He was, though he was still confused, so he nodded yes. She told him, "Well, I'm lost, but if you can help me figure out where I'm at, I know a place where you can get some food."

He went with her, and she took him to a Christian ministry called the Dream Center. Alfred ended up not only getting food but spending a year in a program the Dream Center had for guys just like him. In that program he experienced something he'd never known: a *new* kind of love—unconditional love.

He learned that God was for him and that Jesus liked him, and he surrendered his life to Jesus.

Alfred and I spent an afternoon together, and he showed me what God was doing in South Central LA. Today Alfred oversees efforts to bring eighty tons of food per year to needy people in the area. He started bringing food to rival gangs that were once his sworn enemies. And he eventually accomplished something the city of Los Angeles thought was impossible: he brokered a truce between the three main gangs in the area. Violence dropped off dramatically.

In fact, what Alfred has done has drawn media attention. One article explained that the city had spent tens of millions of dollars and passed all kinds of laws trying to do something about the violence and drug wars but could never do what Alfred did by simply going to the rival gangs with a little food and a lot of love.

It's an unbelievable story. Do you know the star of it? A little old lady who had no sense of direction but who knew that, to live God's will, she had to overcome her fear and walk across an alley to get close to someone who was far from God.

the power
of and

IF YOU HAD TO NARROW IT TO ONE, what emotion would best describe how you feel right now?

Depending on the research you look at, there are anywhere from six to thirty-four thousand emotions you can experience. I won't list all thirty-four thousand here. You probably don't need a list to narrow down how you feel most of the time, anyway. If you're not sure about your emotional state, ask a few of the people you do life with. If they look at you like they're afraid to answer, then *irritable* or *temperamental* may be the diagnosis.

I decided to read through the Gospels to try to determine if there was a primary emotion Jesus felt. He is described as experiencing exhaustion, joy, anger, frustration, disgust, grief, loneliness, rejection, and dread. But the one emotion attributed to Jesus more than any other is *compassion*.

Most of our emotions tend to be self-centered. How we feel is usually determined by what we're experiencing at any given moment. Jesus's primary emotion was determined by what *others* were going through.

Always an *And*

My wife will tell you I can't watch an episode of *Little House on the Prairie* without wiping away a few tears. And my heart is broken when a commercial comes on with images of starving children living in poverty. If I see someone in pain, I feel for them, and for a long time I understood compassion to be a feeling, so I thought of myself as a compassionate person.

But as I traced the times Jesus had compassion in the Gospels, I noticed that a conjunction almost always followed his feeling of compassion. It's not "Jesus had compassion." It's "Jesus had compassion *and . . .*"

In Matthew 20:34, Jesus had compassion on two blind men and touched their eyes. In Mark 1:41, Jesus had compassion on a leper and healed him. In Mark 6:34, Jesus had compassion on the people and began feeding them, and in Matthew 9:35–38, Jesus had compassion on the people and prayed for them.

When Jesus felt compassion, it was followed by action and it always created a story. So many of the one at a time stories in the Gospels start with Jesus's compassion.

More Than Sympathy

Jesus's life makes it clear that compassion isn't just an emotion. It's more than just feeling sorry for someone. Jesus shows us that compassion is a strong emotion that elicits a physical response. The test of compassion is in the *and*.

Over the years, I've taken my son on a number of skiing trips. We usually head to Colorado to hit the slopes for three or four days. I often feel a lot of compassion when I'm skiing through the Colorado Rockies because people are constantly wiping out and taking hard falls.*

The last time we went to Colorado, we began as usual by heading for the lift that would bring us to the top of the mountain. My teenage son, who was already a much better skier than me, listened to my lecture about not going too fast and skiing within his limits. I knew how the day would go: he would speed down the mountain and wait for me at the base, and then we'd take the lift back up together.

When we finally got to the top, we were greeted by slopes with friendly sounding names like Devil's Run, Hell's Canyon, and my personal favorite, Body Bag.

On one of our first runs, my son quickly disappeared out of sight while I skied from side to side, making my way down with what I would call a logical caution based on the titles of those slopes.† About halfway down the mountain, I noticed someone on my left had taken a hard fall. His skis and poles had flown in different directions. Immediately, I felt ~~compassion~~ sympathy. *Poor guy, that's a rough way to start the day.*

---

*Full disclosure: sometimes my compassion may sound more like laughter.
†I believe the official term is "pizza skiing."

The skier was completely laid out, and I could hear him moaning. I hated it on his behalf, but there wasn't much I could do. Then I suddenly realized, *That's my son!* I rushed over to him. He had broken his collarbone and was in a lot of pain.

My response in that moment is the difference between sympathy and compassion. When the wiped-out skier went from being some stranger on the slopes to being my one and only son, it changed everything. I didn't just feel bad for him, I hurt for him. My strong emotion elicited a physical response. I didn't just feel sorry for him, I stopped for him. It was a zoom-lens moment. I was going to do whatever was necessary to help him. Nothing and no one was going to get in my way.

Jesus demonstrated that kind of compassion. *Every* hurting person was his son or daughter. Compassion is the antidote to our indifference.

Eyes-Open Prayer

If compassion is the fuel for living a one at a time life, then how do we grow in compassion? In the next chapter we will talk about some ways to deepen our compassion for hurting and hard-to-love people, but it begins with eyes-open prayer.

I grew up believing there were certain times that were right for prayer. Before meals and at bedtime, of course, and praying at church was also a thing. Also heaving up a desperate Hail Mary prayer before a test you didn't study for was deemed appropriate.

But Jesus's disciples were "constantly" united in prayer, and we are encouraged to "pray without ceasing" (1 Thess. 5:17 ESV) and to "pray at all times" (Eph. 6:18 CSB).

There is a right time to pray—and it is *now*.

Prayer is an expression of our dependence on Jesus, and we're *always* dependent on Jesus, so we always need to be praying. It's a constant connection where we are continually available.

I was also taught there was a right *way* to pray: head bowed and eyes closed. In fact, in our family, if your head wasn't bowed and your eyes weren't closed during prayer, it was considered a serious infraction. When the dinnertime prayer was over, my little sister would start calling out the perps. She was like, "I'm Chris Hansen from NBC. Why don't you have a seat?" The cameras would come out, and they would rewind the tape and show when my eyes were open.

I'd protest, "It was just for a split second!" and counterattack, "How do you know my eyes were open if your eyes were closed?"

At the time, that was the best argument I could come up with, but now I can make a stronger case. If we're supposed to pray "at all times," then we're going to have to pray with our eyes open. Learning to pray with my eyes open changed my relationship with God, but it also changed the way I see people.

This is part of learning to see the world through a zoom lens. As I go through my day and see others one at a time and practice eyes-open prayer, my heart starts to go out to people I would've barely noticed otherwise. Praying with my eyes open helps me see what Jesus saw, feel what Jesus felt, and do what Jesus did.

Lens of Compassion

In Luke 7—the chapter prior to the story where Jesus healed the woman "who could not go unnoticed"—we read about a woman whose son had died.

> Jesus went to a town called Nain, and his disciples and a large crowd went along with him. As he approached the town gate, a dead person was being carried out—the only son of his mother, and she was a widow. And a large crowd from the town was with her. (vv. 11–12)

If we came across a funeral procession with a dead body being carried down the street, it would get our attention because that isn't normal for us. But it was totally normal back then. People died every day. When they died, this is what would happen. The deceased would be carried down the street, people would mourn, and perhaps there would be a mother or father grieving their dead child.

This moment was so ordinary that most people wouldn't have given it a second glance. But eyes-open prayer changes the way we see people in the commonplace moments of life. When you look at your ordinary days through the lens of compassion, you start to see opportunities for God to do something extraordinary through you.

It was just another day, though Luke mentions *two* crowds—one traveling with Jesus, the other with the widow—who come together at the town gate. It's especially crowded, but the throngs of people blurred out and disappeared as Jesus zoomed in on *one* person.

"When the Lord saw her, his heart went out to her and he said, 'Don't cry'" (v. 13). Notice the order of events. First, Jesus saw her. Second, his heart went out to her. There was a connection between what he saw with his eyes and what he felt with his heart. He allowed his heart to engage with what he saw.

Jesus saw this widow grieving her dead son—her only son. In that culture, having no man in her immediate family would've made her desperate and easily dismissed. He didn't just feel sympathy; he felt compassion. His emotion elicited a physical response. He comforted her by telling her, "Don't cry."

That seems like a rookie mistake. We learned in Pastoral Counseling 101 that you don't show up at the funeral home and tell people not to cry. But Jesus could say "don't cry," because he knew what was about to happen.

> Then he went up and touched the bier they were carrying him on, and the bearers stood still. He said, "Young man, I say to you, get up!" The dead man sat up and began to talk, and Jesus gave him back to his mother. (vv. 14–15)

Jesus "touched the bier." Other translations call it a "stretcher," or "open coffin," because they didn't have coffins like we do, with sides and lids. For them, a "coffin" was just a flat piece of wood on which they would lay the dead body.

My guess is that Jesus didn't walk up and touch the wood underneath the body. I think he touched the body.

Either way, this was a crazy moment, because Jesus was crossing boundaries that people *never* crossed. The religious leaders had established over five hundred laws people had to follow. One law was that you couldn't touch a dead body or touch anything a dead body had touched. Dead bodies were considered unclean, and if you touched one, you also became unclean. But Jesus's heart went out to this woman, and he wouldn't let anything stop him from doing what he could to meet her need.

Jesus touched the young man, and I bet the crowd gasped because of how shocking that was. Then something even more incredible happened: the *body* gasped. Jesus's touch brought him back to life.

Don't miss the ripple effect of an act of compassion. We love people one at a time, but doing something for one person has a way of overflowing to others. The son was healed, but something dramatic happened for the mother too.

Back then a widow's only hope was her sons. If a woman had no husband and no sons, it would often lead her to have to do questionable things to generate an income. If she had daughters, she would need more money. Who knows what would become of those daughters? But Jesus touched her son, and he was alive again!

Jesus walked the young man over to his mother and handed him to her. Jesus didn't only give her back her son, he also gave her back her hope, because she had very little just a few moments earlier.

When we pray with our eyes open, *Jesus, help me see people the way you see people*, we'll see what Jesus saw, feel what Jesus felt, and have the opportunity to do something.

Compassion elicits a physical response. The test of compassion is action.

The Bystander Effect

One of the reasons we settle for sympathy instead of acting with compassion is what psychologists call the Bystander Effect. Instead of seeing ourselves as "first responders," we settle for being "concerned bystanders." As concerned bystanders, we can feel good about ourselves for feeling concerned while avoiding the risks of responding. The Bystander Effect has come up more in recent years as a way to explain the phenomenon that unfolds when crowds of people witness and often record something tragic happening, but no one does anything about it.

One especially disturbing example of the Bystander Effect is the story of Kevin Carter.[1] He was a photojournalist who took a famous picture that captured the human suffering in Sub-Saharan Africa. The picture shows a young Sudanese girl. She is weak and alone, trying to crawl to an aid station for food. In the background of the photo is a vulture waiting for her to die.

One version of the story told is that Carter waited some twenty minutes for the vulture to spread its wings because he thought the picture would be better. When that didn't happen, he took the picture without it. It's reported he took the picture then scared the vulture away, but he left the girl because something else caught his eye.

As the picture was seen by more and more people, he started to be asked questions about the girl. What happened to her? Did she get help? Carter couldn't answer those questions. As you might guess, people were severely critical. He tried to explain that people didn't understand what it was like out there. Suffering was everywhere. It surrounded him. He might be able to help the one girl in the photo, but there were thousands more just like her. So, he took a picture but did nothing.

Carter ended up winning a Pulitzer Prize for that photograph, and then he went home and killed himself.

He may have taken the picture, but are we less culpable if we see the picture and read about the suffering and starvation and do nothing?

Of course, we make excuses. There are a few things we commonly say to ourselves to explain why we tend to live our lives as bystanders instead of responders.

"There's nothing I can do."

That's how Kevin Carter felt. There were so many children and the needs were so overwhelming that anything he could do felt meaningless.

In Luke 7, Jesus knew of the pain and suffering taking place around the world in that moment. Jesus knew this woman who lost her son was one of countless others who had lost someone they loved that day. He could've dismissed helping the widow as being too insignificant to make a real difference. But one at a time living focuses on the one person who's in front of us.

Sometimes when we say, "There's nothing I can do," what we're really saying is "I don't know what to do, and whatever I might do won't have much impact." Jesus has power over death and brought this woman's son back to life. We think, *If I had that kind of power, I would do something too. If I had money like Jeff Bezos, or a platform like LeBron, or power like the US president, I would do something, but what can I do?*

Whatever we can do seems too insignificant to make much of a splash. Eugene Peterson calls this "Afghanistanitus." It's the idea that the real opportunities to help people and make a significant difference are in faraway places and extreme situations.

I was driving in my car a month ago and found myself singing a song under my breath. I really wasn't aware I was doing it until my son said, "Umm . . . what are you singing?" I had to stop because I didn't even realize I was singing. It was a silly sounding children's song* about God's love I had learned as a grade schooler. I hadn't thought about that song or sung it in decades. My son asked if it was a real song and where I'd learned it.

I grew up in a neighborhood where Mrs. Knapp, a small elderly widow, lived a few streets down. Mrs. Knapp always had a smile on her face and a freezer full of popsicles. Those cheap "tear the wrapper open with your teeth and push it up from the bottom" kind. I'm not sure how it started, but somehow every kid in the neighborhood knew they were always welcome to stop by Mrs. Knapp's house for a popsicle. We would ride our bikes over, and she would invite us in and let us eat a popsicle on the floor of her family room.

Most of the time, as we ate our popsicles, she would open up a Bible story book and read us a short story. She

*"*Give me umption for my gumption, help me function, function, function.*" If you know, you know.

would also teach us a corny but catchy song about Jesus. Mrs. Knapp may have never felt like she was doing much, but I wonder how many other middle-aged men who grew up in that neighborhood still remember songs about God's love and stories about Jesus because of an elderly widow who kept a freezer full of Fla-Vor-Ice.

"Somebody else will do something."

You're praying with your eyes open and see someone right in front of you in need, but you're sure someone else will do something.

Imagine reading in the news about a young lady assaulted in the middle of the day in a parking lot. According to the report, no less than ten people witnessed the assault. In fact, a number of the witnesses pulled out their phones and recorded it, but no one did anything. No one stepped in. No one intervened. No one even called the police.

When the witnesses were interviewed, they all expressed concern and showed sympathy for what happened to the young lady. But why did no one act? There were so many people in the parking lot that they all assumed someone else would help. Everyone assumed someone would do something, so no one did anything.

Someone else will stop and check on that homeless person. Someone else will sponsor that child. Someone else will check on that coworker who hasn't been heard from lately. Someone else will do something about those trafficked women. Someone else will take in those foster children. Someone else will make sure those kids in the neighborhood have a place to feel safe and loved.

There's one other reason why we live as bystanders instead of responders. We would never say this out loud and probably not even to ourselves. But if we were brutally honest we would admit . . .

"I just don't care that much."

Most of us feel compassionate generally because we're sure we're not the opposite of that. We tend to think the opposite of compassion is hatred, and we know we don't feel that.

But if you check a thesaurus, you'll find the opposite of compassion is *not* hatred. It's indifference or apathy. Instead of seeing, we look the other way. If compassion is reaching out with an open hand, the opposite of compassion is not to hit with a closed fist. The opposite of compassion is putting your hands in your pockets, shrugging your shoulders, walking away, and saying to yourself, *It's not my problem.*

The late preacher Fred Craddock pointed out that the early church leaders understood just how dangerous the spirit of indifference was in the life of believers.[2] Many years ago, before there was much biblical literature and before the average person could read, these leaders got together and came up with a list of sins that have come to be known as "The Seven Deadly Sins." Those seven sins don't appear as a list anywhere in the Bible, but after studying the Scriptures they put it together to help people know what not to do.

Most of the sins on that list are what we might expect, but one that might seem out of place is the sin of *sloth.* Sloth doesn't seem very deadly. It sounds like spending too much time lying out by the pool.

In its original Latin, the word is *acedia,* and sloth isn't actually a very helpful translation. A more accurate translation would be "without care" or "I don't care." It is dangerous and deadly for a person to reach a point where they're so jaded and calloused that they're indifferent to the hurting people around them.

Compelled by Compassion

In Nain, Jesus had *no* earthly connection to the funeral procession. He technically wasn't acquainted with any of the people. The mourners weren't his friends or family. Jesus didn't know the people, and the people didn't ask him to get involved. No one asked him for help. It was his compassion that compelled him.

A while back I was in the checkout line at Walmart. Typically, I spend the majority of my time in checkout lines looking at the other lines to see which one I should've chosen because it's moving faster. But as I had been trying to pray with eyes open for the people around me, this time I noticed a young lady in front of me holding a baby. I didn't know her or even her name, but I started to pray silently for her. *God, I know this young mom is your daughter and you love her. Please let her know you love her, and if there is anything you want me to do for your daughter, please let me know.*

As the cashier was ringing up her items, I overheard her tell the cashier to stop because that was her limit. She then asked the cashier to take a few items back off so she would have enough money. I didn't want her to feel embarrassed, so I took a step back and pretended to look at the candy and gift cards on the aisle. I said another prayer for her: *God, would you please provide for her today. Would you please lead someone who knows about her situation to do something to help this young mom.*

Yeah, I can be a little slow.

Then, of course, it hit me: *I* knew about the situation and *I* could reach out and *I* could help. By this time she had paid and was gone, leaving me staring straight at the gift cards. I quickly bought one, hustled out to the parking lot, and found her putting her groceries in her car. I handed her the gift card and said, "Hey! I'm pretty sure Jesus wanted me to give this to you." I could tell from her reaction that she was touched.

As I walked to my car, I felt so convicted. I can only imagine how many thousands of opportunities like that I have missed because I had settled for sympathy over compassion.

Beyond Good Intentions

I've been hearing recently about the growing popularity of wearing workout clothes without having any intention of actually working out. The trend has created a new category of clothing called *athleisure*.* It's a seventy-*billion*-dollar industry and growing.

Why? People like to wear running shoes and running clothes but don't like to run. Similarly, the sale of yoga clothes has outpaced people who actually do yoga by more than a hundredfold.

*It's a combination of the words *athletics* and *leisure*. It's interesting that athleisure contains one-third of the word *athletics* but all of *leisure*.

loving one at a time

Apparently people love these clothes because they're comfortable but don't love working out because then they're uncomfortable. There's something about wearing workout clothes that makes you feel more like you've done something—but you haven't.

The feeling of compassion is like that. It can make you feel like you've done something when you haven't. The dangerous myth we can fall into is thinking *I am compassionate because I* feel *compassionate*. For example,

> I watch TV late at night and a commercial comes on for Feed the Children. I see those images and I'm so compassionate it makes my stomach churn.
>
> I watch the evening news and see people facing injustice because of their skin color. I'm compassionate because that makes me angry.
>
> I watch a movie where a mother is dying of cancer and has to say goodbye to her children. I'm compassionate because it makes me tear up.

Researchers at the University of British Columbia have done studies that demonstrate people who show support for their favorite causes on social media are *less* likely to donate money or volunteer their time. They feel compassionate and, apparently, that feeling is enough.[3]

There's something about *feeling* compassionate that makes you feel like you *are* compassionate, but nope. That's not biblical compassion.

Technically, *compassion* is defined as "a deep awareness or any sympathy for another's suffering."[4] It's a noun, but

Christians need to redefine it as a verb. That means there should always be an *and*. As in, *I feel compassionate* and *I then act*. Real compassion doesn't just break your heart. It moves your muscles.

Feelings of compassion are God's call to action. The way you know whether you chose compassion isn't by how you feel but by what you *do*. The test of compassion isn't the feelings you have but the one at a time stories you can tell.

extra mile mentality

I AM NOT SAYING I'm an attorney. I mean, I didn't go to law school. I did, however, watch a bunch of episodes of *Law & Order*. I even took notes. I walked into the courtroom ready to yell, "I object!" and to whisper, "Can I approach the bench, your honor?" with a knowing look.

Why? Because I was being sued and I was determined to win.

The accusation on the lawsuit wasn't true, and I immediately became defensive. I was being falsely accused, and I was ready to stand up for my rights.

I called an attorney friend of mine and asked what he thought I should do. He said, "Oh, man, this is small claims court. You definitely want to just offer a settlement. You don't want to have to spend a day in a courtroom defending yourself. Just offer a settlement and be done with it. That's probably what they're expecting anyway."

I told him that was really good advice and thanked him for his counsel. I then hung up the phone and loudly proclaimed, "Not a chance!"

That's when I started binge-watching *Law & Order*.

I bought a briefcase and a plane ticket. I stepped in the courtroom. If only Dick Wolf* could see me now. I made my case, taking a stand for my rights. The judge declared I won. I didn't have to pay anything. I walked out of the courtroom feeling pretty good about myself. *No one was going to take advantage of me!*

Looking back though . . . I'm not sure I did the right thing. I wonder if I did what Jesus would have done.

God's Dream for Your Life

Jesus's most famous sermon is called "The Sermon on the Mount." Another title for it could be "God's Dream for Your Life." In it, Jesus teaches God's plan for us. We've been looking at examples of how Jesus impacted one person at a time, but in the Sermon on the Mount Jesus gave some core teachings that laid the foundation for one at a time living. Specifically, Jesus raised the bar on how we are to treat others.

Jesus reframed how we are to look at and treat people who are difficult to love. Six times he referenced what people had previously been taught by saying, "You have heard that it was said." That was a common rabbinical phrase typically used when a rabbi was going to reference a teaching from the Old Testament law, called the Torah.

*Executive producer of *Law & Order*.

So, Jesus was pointing out commonly understood and widely accepted teachings from Scripture. It would be like me saying, "I know you were taught in school," or "I know your parents may have said," or "The church you grew up in may have believed . . ."

Jesus began with, "You have heard that it was said," and everyone there would have nodded at his quote—then he surprised them with the next word, *but*. He then said, "But I tell you" and introduced a new standard of how to relate to others. He wasn't contradicting the law; he was clarifying it and giving a deeper understanding of what God wanted for humankind when the law was given.

Let's walk through some of Jesus's Sermon on the Mount teachings to help us better understand the one at a time life. But before we begin, I need to warn you that some of Jesus's teachings here will be hard to receive. This was true then but even more so today.

What Jesus teaches contradicts the way most of us think. His teaching will challenge your innate perspective and cultural understanding when it comes to your relationships.

As you read this chapter, you will probably feel defensive at times. You will think of a person or situation in your life and begin to justify and rationalize. What Jesus asks will go against your instinct. Living the one at a time life may feel unnatural or uncomfortable at first. But Jesus makes it clear that if you align your life and relationships with his way of treating people, two things will happen.

First, **you will be blessed.** The Sermon on the Mount starts with a series of statements that begin with this promise: "Blessed are . . ." Everyone I know wants to live a blessed and happy life, but the path that leads there will often feel like it's taking you in the opposite direction. What Jesus teaches may seem counterintuitive and the opposite of what you think will make you happy, but it will bless your life and the lives of those around you.

Second, **you will make a difference.** Everyone I know wants to be blessed *and* wants to make a difference in this world. In Matthew 5, Jesus tells his followers we are the salt of the earth and the light of the world (see vv. 13–14), then teaches us how to treat people in a way that shines a light and adds some salt.

In those days salt served a number of purposes. It was used to preserve food but also as we commonly use it today, to add flavor. I think we can all agree that some things are not good without some salt, like a baked potato or corn on the cob. No offense, but if you eat corn on the cob without salt, I don't trust you. You've got to salt your cob. If you're on a date with someone who orders corn on the cob, that's a red flag, but if they don't salt it, just get up and leave.

Treating people the way Jesus teaches will add salt, but when we *don't* treat people this way, it's like corn on the cob without salt—nobody is interested. If we apply his one at a time approach to the people in our lives, Jesus says it will make God look good, and people will notice and get an appetite for God (see v. 16).

Default Setting

What's your default setting when it comes to dealing with difficult people? The bully at school. The rude coworker.

The steamrolling sibling. The annoying neighbor. The ungrateful child. The selfish friend.

How do your respond when someone hurts you? Betrays you? Rejects you? Ridicules you? Takes advantage of you? Gossips about you?

Jesus said, "You have heard that it was said, 'Eye for eye, and tooth for tooth'" (v. 38).

Yeah, I've heard that. And I *like* that. You hit me, I'll hit you back. You yell at me, I'll yell back. I'm not going to raise my voice first, but if you raise your voice, I'm going to raise my voice back. You call me names, I'll call you names. You honk at me, I'll honk back. Like, before your honk is even done honkin', I've already started to honk. I'll honk over the top of your honk and won't stop honkin' until your honk stops. I will out-honk you every time, bro!

I'm comfortable—I think *we're* comfortable—with an "eye for an eye" approach. It appeals to our sense of justice.

Jesus was referencing a widely known Old Testament law: "Eye for an eye." It's known as the principle of exact retribution, and it seems to make a lot of sense. It addresses injustice in such a way that people will be discouraged from hurting and doing wrong to others. This law also kept things from escalating so conflicts didn't turn into the Hatfields and McCoys. The punishment or retribution shouldn't exceed the offense.

Jesus may have begun by saying, "You have heard that it was said, 'Eye for eye,'" but then he gave a new standard: "But I tell you, do not resist an evil person" (v. 39). Jesus has a way of challenging people by making a broad statement and then getting personal with specific examples that make people really uncomfortable. Here he gave four different scenarios to help paint a picture of what it looks like to not resist an evil person.

Scenario #1: "If anyone slaps you on the right cheek, turn to them the other cheek also" (v. 39).

When my wife and I were first married, we lived in a small, cheap house. How small? Right around seven hundred square feet. How cheap? Our house payment was $213 a month.*

The walls were paper thin, and our neighbor had a dog that was constantly barking. The dog. Never. Stopped. Barking. Even writing about it twenty-five years later spikes my adrenaline. That dog would bark incessantly at night, and the thin walls made it sound like it was in the ~~room~~ bed with us. I would wake up and check under the covers. We would lie in bed staring at the ceiling. Eventually the barking would pause, and we would fall asleep, but it seemed like that would cue the dog to start barking again.

I tried to find nice ways to mention to our neighbor that his dog was barking while we were trying to sleep, but he would just nod his head. It was like he was acknowledging what I was saying but not taking any responsibility. The dog kept barking. We kept not sleeping.

I complained about this at a family gathering, and my uncle offered an exact retribution solution. When he said it, I didn't take it seriously.

Then one night I had enough. Before I tell you what I did, remember this was before cell phones and caller

*That is not a typo. I did not forget a 0 at the end. It was $213.

ID. I picked up the phone in the middle of the night and called the neighbor. He answered, half asleep, clearly unfazed by all the barking. I think it was like white noise for him. The moment he sleepily said, "Hello," I started barking as loud as I could into the receiver. I'm not going to lie; it felt good. It seemed like the right thing to do. You bark at me, I'll bark back. That's how "eye for an eye" works.

But Jesus said that instead of retaliating, if someone slaps you on the right cheek, offer them your other cheek.†
The fact that Jesus said "right cheek" is significant, because if someone slaps you on the right cheek and they're right-handed, what are they doing? They're coming at you with a backhand. In that culture and in that time, that was especially disrespectful and insulting. There was actually a different penalty for slapping somebody with a backhand versus a forehand.

So, is there someone in your life who seems to have it out for you? Maybe it's a neighbor who is always provoking you. Or a family member who's always antagonizing you. Or a coworker who is always passive-aggressive. What happens when they walk in the room? Immediately

†Context is important here. Jesus is not talking about spousal or other domestic abuse. Jesus said it would be better for those kinds of abusers to have a heavy stone hung on their neck and be thrown into the sea. If you are in a relationship and being physically abused, you need to find a safe place and get help. If you don't know where to go or what to do, please go to the website of the church where I am a pastor, www .southeastchristian.org. On the front page is a button you can click to ask for help, and we will help you. Or you can call (502) 253-8000 anytime, day or night, and you will be connected to a pastor who will know how to help you. You are God's child and you are my family. You are not alone.

your spirit goes into a *Cobra Kai* fighting stance. *Mercy is for the weak!*

That may feel right, but what Jesus teaches us to do is counterintuitive. When someone treats you with disrespect, turn to them your other cheek—in other words, don't get so easily offended, or don't mouth off, side-eye, or check out. You won't feel like it. But if you do this, it will bless your life and impact others. People will notice, and it will make God look good.

Scenario #2: "And if anyone wants to sue you and take your shirt, hand over your coat as well" (v. 40).

Wait, wait, wait. Jesus, you said if someone slaps you on the cheek, don't retaliate but turn to them the other cheek. I don't like it, but I can live with that sting. Now you're saying if someone sues me for the shirt off my back, I'm to give my coat as well? *Whaaa?* Should I go ahead and put that in a nice little gift bag while I'm at it? This isn't just a pacifistic approach of turning the other cheek. Are you saying I should return cruelty with kindness?

In those days, people might have several shirts but typically only *one* coat. When it was cold at night, that coat became a blanket. Exodus 22 essentially says everyone has a right to a coat, since it was needed for protection from the elements. Because having a coat was considered to be a basic human right, a person wasn't permitted to sue someone for their coat. But . . . sometimes following Jesus means letting go of our rights. Sometimes letting go of our rights is the righteous thing to do.

I thought about this and realized I might be willing to give up my coat for someone I love. For instance, my grandmother. I would rather be cold than have her be cold. Besides, if I gave her my coat, she would pay me back in homemade cinnamon rolls. Deal!

Most people would probably be willing to give their coat to someone they love and who would do something nice for them in return. But give up your coat for someone who is suing you? No thanks. No one does that.

And that's the point. The world will notice that kind of response.

It makes me think back to that lawsuit. I'm still impressed with my lawyer skills, but when I read what Jesus said here, I look back and realize I missed an opportunity. I had never met the person who was suing me. I don't remember the name of the plaintiff. I don't remember ever praying for them. I don't know if they knew Jesus or if they were part of a church.

I assume they googled my name before they sued me and knew I was a pastor. I wonder if they'd ever had an interaction with a pastor. I know I was innocent of what I was accused of, but if I had it to do over again, I would reach out to them and listen to their perspective.

I wonder . . . what if I saw the person suing me as a one at a time opportunity rather than my opposition? If I hadn't been so quick to defend myself and stand up for my rights, would it have been possible to add some salt?

Scenario #3: "If anyone forces you to go one mile, go with them two miles" (v. 41).

Here's the problem I have with this: *forces*. If someone *asks* me to go one mile, yeah, okay. I don't really feel like it, but I probably still need to get my steps in, so I'll go a mile with you if you ask me. But the minute I feel forced, my pride kicks in. I get sensitive and angry, because *force* implies someone is trying to control me.

There was this law back then that Roman soldiers could force civilians into acts of service, but there were limitations. A Roman soldier could force a Jew to carry his pack for one mile, but not any farther. The Jewish person didn't have an option, so they'd pick up the pack and carry it a mile, but not another step. They couldn't be forced into a second mile.

Roman soldiers were the enemy. They treated Jewish people like dogs. So, imagine this scenario: a Jewish man is coming home from work. He's tired and hungry and just wants to get home in time for a little SportsCenter before going to bed. He sees a soldier on the side of the road. *Oh, great.* This is the last thing he needs.

The soldier throws his pack onto the ground in front of the man's feet and says, "Be a good dog and carry this for me."

The Jewish man is angry and upset every step of the way. As soon as he hits a mile, he drops the pack and marches home. What happens when he gets home? Still frustrated and angry, he slams the door, yells at his wife, is short with the kids, kicks the dog, and spends the rest of the evening in his room.

But what if he got to the end of the first mile and said to the Roman soldier, "You know what? I don't mind going a second mile if that would help you out."

It feels like that's giving up power, but if you think about it, isn't he taking some control back? No one is making him do it; he's *choosing* it. He might come home a little later than he had planned, but he walks in the door with dignity.

My guess is the Roman soldier wouldn't have known what to say. I'm sure he would have told the other soldiers about it. "You wouldn't believe what happened to me today. I made a Jew carry my pack one mile, and he voluntarily carried it two." People would've noticed.

Jesus teaches his followers to have a second mile mentality with one person at a time, even when that person is an enemy who is making your life miserable. What would it look like to live that way today?

Try this. If someone insults you, say something nice to them. If your spouse criticizes you, compliment them. If someone blames you, bless them. If your server is short with you, give a more generous tip than you would normally give.

You don't think they'd notice that? If the boss is especially grumpy and demanding, pray for her and drop a note of encouragement. Go the second mile. It'll bless your life. It will make a difference in this world, and it will make God look good.

Scenario #4: "Give to the one who asks you, and do not turn away from the one who wants to borrow from you" (v. 42).

Do you have some people in your life who always need something from you and are always asking? When you see them coming, you know they're going to have a story of what's wrong and what they want from you to help them feel better. They never seem to have anything to give you emotionally. They are like a sponge—always taking but never giving anything back. They quickly soak up whatever emotional energy you might have.

How do you respond to that?

A few years ago, I was visiting with a member of our church who owns a local business. There had recently been an incident where a young man came into his store and stole something that was worth about two hundred bucks. The owner was upset and angry when he realized what had happened. When he reviewed the security cameras, he was able to get a license plate number, and soon he had a name. We will call him Jake. The owner called the police with Jake's name and picture, and the police took a report, but what happened next was mostly up to the store owner.

He considered his options. He could take the "eye for an eye" approach and make Jake pay for what he had done. Jake was facing up to a thousand-dollar fine and a year in jail. The store owner didn't want to ruin this young man's life, so he considered a second option. After Jake returned the item, he could sit him down and yell at him, venting his anger. That's what he wanted to do. That's what felt right.

The store owner, however, is a follower of Jesus and decided on a third option. He took time to pray for Jake and ask God what he should do. That night he left Jake a message and asked him to come by the store. The next day Jake's father came by the store with the stolen item. He apologized on behalf of his son. He asked the store owner not to press charges and offered some money to help make things right. He also explained that his son had some addiction struggles.

The store owner appreciated the father stopping by but said he really wanted Jake to come by the store. The next day Jake came and apologized. The store owner told Jake, "I forgive you and I care about you. I won't press charges; the only thing I'm going to ask is for you to come to church with me."

Jake agreed and came to church the next weekend. Our church was able to help Jake get connected to an inpatient treatment center for his addiction, and he started down the road to recovery.

Sometime later Jake's sister stopped by the store and introduced herself. She told the store owner that she and her husband often came to our church and had invited Jake and their parents, but they had never shown any interest. But recently they had all started coming together.

What changed? Well, the store owner put some salt on it.

One Extra Mile at a Time

Maybe, when you hear this teaching of Jesus, you think, *Who does that? Who gets hit and turns the other cheek? Who gets sued and hands over their coat? Who gets forced to go one mile and then volunteers a second? I can see why it would make a difference, but who actually lives that way?*

Jesus.

He was *always* doing this. Philippians 2 says when we consider others better than ourselves and put their needs ahead of our own, we are following the example of Jesus, who made himself nothing and took on the nature of a servant.

Then, at the end of his earthly life, Jesus, the Son of God, was falsely accused. He was unjustly arrested. He was violently beaten. A soldier blindfolded him. Another slapped him. Another spit in his face. He was brutally mocked.

One of the soldiers said, "If you're a prophet, then tell us which one of us hit you" (see Mark 14:65). The irony of course is that Jesus knew. He knew the soldier's name. He knew the number of hairs on that soldier's head.

Jesus was slapped, but he didn't slap back. He could've. Don't mistake his love for weakness. There may have been a garrison of soldiers abusing him that day, but in Matthew 26:52–54, Jesus makes it clear that if he wanted, he could command twelve legions of angels. If you're a little rusty on your first-century math, twelve legions adds up to seventy-two thousand angels.

With every insult hurled, with every punch thrown, with every crack of the whip, with every cry of agony, with every drop of blood shed, seventy-two thousand angels grew more restless. All Jesus had to do was say the word and this would all be over.

But Jesus didn't need the angels' help. With a blink of his eyes, he could have struck the soldiers all blind. A nod of his head had the power to leave them all paralyzed. One word from his mouth could curse every last one of them to hell.

Finally, after he was nailed to the cross, he spoke for the first time since his ordeal began. All of heaven's armies leaned forward, ready for him to give the command.

What did he say? "Father, forgive them" (Luke 23:34). He prayed that God would forgive his enemies.

It's hard to think of it this way, but when you're mistreated and taken advantage of, it provides an opportunity to love and live like Jesus.

We'd prefer to change the world one social media post at a time, but it's more likely that your greatest impact will come one offense at a time, one insult at a time, one irritation at a time, one aggravation at a time, one extra mile at a time.

don't be a prig*

I HAVE A COLLEGE FRIEND named Caleb.[1]

His parents, both college professors, divorced when Caleb was only two years old. They each announced they were gay. Caleb's mother fell in love with a woman at work. Caleb's father fell in love with a man at work.

Caleb grew up going to gay pride parades and rallies. When he was nine, he was marching in a pride parade in Kansas City with his mom and her partner, Vera, when he saw a man throw a cup of urine on Vera.

Caleb, stunned, asked his mom, "Why would that man do that?" His mother told him, "Because he's a Christian, and Christians hate people."

That was how Caleb was introduced to Christianity and, unfortunately, it wasn't the last negative experience he had with angry and self-righteous Christians.

When Caleb was sixteen, two buddies invited him to a Bible study. Caleb was excited. He despised Christians and

*A prig is a self-righteous person who behaves as if superior to others.

thought this was his chance to finally let them know. The person leading that Bible study was Joe Weece. I know Joe. He is a man who lives out the one at a time way of Jesus.

It didn't take long for Caleb to become disruptive in that Bible study. He was mean-spirited. He tried to disprove everything Joe said. He did everything he could to pick a fight, but Joe was always gracious to him.

Caleb's two friends didn't get mad or defensive either. In fact, they consistently returned his anger with kindness.

Caleb was surprised and, over time, grew to really like and respect the guys in that group. He wondered if maybe he had met the one odd group of Christians who were misrepresenting the hate-filled Christianity Jesus intended and Caleb had experienced. He decided to find out by going to the source.

He started reading the Bible and eventually got to the story in John 8 where a woman caught in the act of adultery is thrown at Jesus's feet by men who wanted him to condemn her so they could stone her to death.

Caught and Brought

We don't know a lot about that woman.

We know she was married. The Mishnah (the oral tradition of Jewish laws) called for a single woman who slept with a married man to be strangled to death, but a woman who was married and committed adultery was to be stoned to death.

She was married, which means at some point she had been a young bride with dreams of having a husband who loved her, dreams of how they would raise their children together. Whatever her hopes and dreams might have been, they didn't include what was happening to her on this day. This was a nightmare.

Where things started to go wrong is hard to say, but we could probably guess. She was disappointed in her marriage. It might have been her husband's fault or might have been hers—probably it was some of both.

She was married, but she felt so lonely. That may seem impossible, but if you know, you know. Somewhere along the line, she met another man. He noticed her, wanted to listen to her. It was what her aching heart longed for.

At first it was all quite innocent, and then one day they crossed a line, and then another line, and she kept crossing lines until finally she ended up in bed with this man. She told herself it was a one-time thing and would never happen again. But it happened again, and then again. She couldn't seem to bring herself to cut things off.

She started living with this secret. It was like she had two different lives. It was a constant weight she carried. I bet it was killing her. Living a lie. The fear that people would find out. The guilt and shame because . . . God knew. Everything she had been taught about God by the religious leaders of her day led her to assume that God surely hated her because of her sin.

Then one day it happened. She was in bed with him, again, and suddenly there were eyes staring at her. They were the hard, flinty eyes of the religious leaders of the town. These men were well known.

She had seen them many times around town, giving disapproving stares to anyone they considered beneath them, which was everyone. The problem is that this time they weren't around town; they were in her bedroom, and their angry and hateful stares were for her. And she was not only beneath them; she was in bed beneath a man who was not her husband. She was caught.

The man was just as guilty, just as caught, but they left him alone. They grabbed her and pulled her out of the room. She screamed in fear. She tried to reach for clothes, for a bedsheet, for anything to cover her nakedness.

Suddenly, she was being marched across town for all to see, a parade of shame, her confusion and humiliation increasing with every step.

She realized they were taking her to the temple. A torrent of thoughts must have inundated her mind. *Why are they taking me to the temple? Are they going to bring me inside? Will they kill me? In the temple?*

But then they stopped just outside it, in the temple courts. Humiliated and embarrassed, she kept her eyes down. She heard one of the men speak. We have his words recorded in the book of John: "Teacher, this woman was caught in the act of adultery. In the Law Moses commanded us to stone such women. Now what do you say?" (8:4–5).

She realized their intention *was* to kill her.

She looked up with panicked eyes and frantically surveyed the scene and saw *him*. The one who was being asked this question that would determine whether she lived or died. As was often the case, there was a crowd gathered around him.

This man knelt down and started writing on the ground, in the dirt, with his finger. He seemed to be ignoring them. He wouldn't answer their question.

What is he doing? She tried to make out the words he was writing in the dirt.

The religious leaders, who wouldn't loosen their grip on her now-throbbing arms, continued to question the man, demanding he condemn her.

Choosing Condemnation

Can I ask you a kind of awkward personal question?

Who are you tempted to condemn? To write off? To blame for your hurt? To shame for their sin?

If there was someone, or a group of someones, whom you could grab and bring to God and accuse, who would it be? Who is the person you wouldn't mind throwing stones at, one at a time?

Like the religious leaders, maybe you find yourself dealing with some self-righteous anger. Sometimes that anger comes from something someone has done to us. Depending on who did what, you may find that you're full of anger not only at the person who did it but everybody else too. Anger is a cancer that spreads.

Oftentimes the self-righteous anger that these religious leaders had came not from something that was done to them but something they did. When we feel guilty about our own sins and struggles, that guilt often comes to the surface in anger. And anger has a way of boiling up and spilling out on the people around us—and then those people become angry, and on it goes.

Recently I was reading some research on the growing problem of road rage. We've become more and more angry with each other. One of the reasons for this increase is what psychologists call the anger-bandwagon effect. Anger is often contagious. One angry person can make the people around them angry too.

Anger, like love, has a way of spreading one person at a time. One person in the family is constantly angry, and the rest of the family is more on edge. One angry person at work spreads negativity throughout the office. One angry person starts venting on social media, and other people get riled up and join in.

When we hold on to bitterness and anger toward a person, it has a way of leaking out and infecting our other relationships. The term for this is *transference*. Our resentment toward a parent can cause us to have misplaced anger toward our spouse. Anger that we feel toward a coworker has a way of following us home and transferring over to our kids.

Your anger toward the people who have hurt you builds a wall around your heart that doesn't just keep those people at a safe distance but keeps everyone else away as well.

So, who makes you angry?

The spouse who cheated on you?
The child who broke your heart?
The contractor who swindled you?
The business partner who lied to you?
The relative who made you feel so unimportant grow-
    ing up?
Your boss?
Your employee?

Those Democrats?

Those Republicans?

The neighbor with the dog that won't stop barking?

The reason you're inclined to condemn them is because there's something about them you don't like. Right?

Or there's something about them that subconsciously reminds you of something you don't like about yourself. There's a way they think, or act, or talk, or treat people that you hate, and it makes you angry. There's something they did, or something they're doing, that keeps them off your one at a time list.

In their anger, these self-righteous religious leaders had become experts in judging, rejecting, and condemning people one at a time.

Question: *Has condemning a person ever changed that person?*

It's a significant question. Have you ever met someone who told you, "Well, I was always this certain way, but then I met this hate-filled person who made me feel condemned, and that's when my whole life changed!"

No, you haven't. Me neither.

Another question: *Has feeling condemned ever helped you to change?* Has condemnation ever led you to transformation? I bet not, because that's not the way it works. Romans 2:4 says it's kindness that leads us to repentance.

Angrily pointing out a person's sins doesn't lead them out of those sins. Don't confuse your bitterness and hatred with showing tough love. Loathing doesn't lead to life change.

In the Sermon on the Mount, Jesus talked about how we are to treat others and warned against the seriousness of anger. Just because you can't see it doesn't mean it's not a big deal. Jesus also did something rather shocking: he put people who have anger in their hearts in the same circle as murderers. In Matthew 5:21, Jesus said, "You have heard that it was said to the people long ago, 'You shall not murder, and anyone who murders will be subject to judgment.'"

People would look at that and say, "Well, I would never murder anyone." You might hear someone defend themselves by saying, "It's not like I killed anybody." So, you feel good about yourself because you're not a murderer.

Everyone can agree with the command, "Thou shall not murder."* But then Jesus expanded the circle in verse 22: "But I tell you that anyone who is angry with a brother or sister will be subject to judgment."

Jesus was making the point that you can't compare yourself to a murderer and feel good about yourself if you have anger in your heart toward someone in your life. I have never murdered anyone, but there have been many times over the years where I've become angry and ex-pressed my anger in hurtful ways—raising my voice, calling names, being disrespectful, gossiping about the person.

Our tendency is to dismiss these things as no big deal. Everyone gets a little carried away now and then.

*If you come across someone who disagrees with it, my suggestion is to run away. Don't get into a debate with someone who takes the stance that "murder is always an option."

Some of you get angry, but you don't yell or call names. You're not the type to pick up a rock and throw it at someone. Instead, you withdraw, you go silent. Not as a way to collect yourself but to hurt the other person. You know full well your ongoing silence and passive-aggressive spirit are driven by anger.

One of my friends, when he starts to get angry, will say, "Here's the thing . . ." If he says, "Here's the thing," he is also going to look at you with a smile—but make no mistake, it's an angry smile. He murders with a smile on his face.

Another friend of mine will say, whenever she's angry, "I just find it funny . . ." If she starts a sentence that way, just know what she's about to say is *not* something she found funny, and you'd better not laugh.*

Releasing Rocks

These religious leaders were angry and full of self-righteous hatred as they dragged this woman before Jesus, who had been sitting there teaching but then started writing on the ground. As the story unfolds, we get to see contrast between the one at a time way of Jesus and the one at a time way of the religious leaders.

We don't know why Jesus was writing on the ground or what he was writing. Different Bible scholars have different theories. The one thing we do know is that by writing on the ground, he took the condemning eyes of the woman's accusers off of her.

*And by "friend" I mean "wife." When she reads this footnote, she will say, "I just find it funny . . ."

Why would Jesus have wanted to do that? Because she was his *daughter*, God's daughter. She was ashamed and devastated. Jesus was (and is) full of compassion.

The accusers waited for the condemnation they were hoping for, then Jesus finally looked up and said, "Let any one of you who is without sin be the first to throw a stone at her" (John 8:7).

She must have thought, *That's it, my death sentence.*

Because these men were known for being sinless. And in case there was any doubt, just ask them, and they'd be happy to tell you. She held her breath and waited for the first stone to strike her.

But instead it struck the ground. One of the religious leaders had dropped his stone. Then another. And another. And another. And another.

The hands that held her so firmly released their grip. The men all walked away. We're not sure why. Some speculate that the words Jesus wrote in the dirt were a list of sins they had committed. Maybe. Perhaps when they knew that Jesus knew, they dropped their stones. We don't know.

We do know that she must have been confused by what had happened. She didn't know what to do. She just stood there. I bet in her head it was like she was trying to solve a math problem.

Apparently, only someone without sin could judge someone else for his or her sin. And so, since it turned out that all her accusers actually *had* sinned, there was no one who could judge or punish her for her wrongdoing.

Well, there was one. The man who had been writing in the dirt looked up at her. "Woman, where are they?" he asked. "Has no one condemned you?" (v. 10).

She had just been caught in the act of adultery. She was standing naked in front of a man who apparently had some kind of authority over even the religious authorities. And he was speaking to her.

"No one, sir," she answered (v. 11).

She still wasn't sure what was happening, but she saw something in his eyes. Compassion. His eyes were full of compassion. He spoke again. "Then neither do I condemn you. . . . Go now and leave your life of sin" (v. 11).

It's an incredible story and so similar to so many stories we see in the Gospels. With Jesus, every story of destruction has a chance to end in celebration.

With Jesus, something broken can become beautiful. One story at a time, as one person at a time discovers grace and forgiveness when they deserve judgment and expect punishment.

The religious leaders of Jesus's day who were condemning this woman kept an unofficial list of what sins were acceptable and what sins were unacceptable. They put people into two different circles. One circle was for people whose sins were considered "no big deal." The other was for people whose sins were considered a "really big deal." The people in that circle were judged, shamed, and condemned.

The religious leaders seemed to use two primary criteria to determine which sin was put in which circle.

The first criteria: *Is it something people can see?* They were obsessed with appearance but not so concerned with authenticity. So, they would tolerate and look the other way when it came to sins of the heart. We are not so different. I can tell you as a pastor I've rarely had anyone confess the sin of greed, jealousy, discontentment, impatience, anger, or pride. If no one can see it or find out about it, we think it's not that big of a deal.

The second criteria: *Is it something I don't struggle with?* For them, and still for us today, there's a tendency to be hypercritical and judgmental of people whose struggle is different from our own.

The woman's condemners thought her sin defined her, that she *was* her worst mistake. They believed that by holding her up before Jesus and the crowd, everyone would see that her transgression diluted her value, that it made her disposable and unwantable.

Pastor Matt Chandler tells about being a freshman in Bible college and becoming friends with a young, single mom with a rough past named Kim.[2] She didn't know Jesus, but Matt and some of his buddies were beginning to share their faith with her. They invited her to a Christian concert.

After the band played, a preacher went on stage and announced he would be talking about sex. He held up a beautiful rose and said, "This rose is perfect. It smells amazing. Everyone needs to see, touch, and smell this rose."

He tossed it into the crowd, and it was passed around, as the preacher spoke in an angry tone about sexual sin and promiscuity. At the end of his sermon, he invited the person holding the rose to bring it up on stage. The rose was broken, with petals and leaves missing. The preacher said, "Now, who wants a rose like this? It's been passed all around. Everybody's touched it. It's no longer a pure rose. Who would want a rose like this? *Nobody* wants a rose like this!"

A week or two later, Matt hadn't seen Kim in class. He was worried about her and left a few messages. Eventually he got a call from Kim's mom letting him know that Kim had been in a bad car accident and was in the hospital. When Matt went to see her in the hospital, they talked for a few minutes, but in the middle of the conversation she blurted out a question: "Do you think I'm a dirty rose?"

Matt said his heart sank, and he began to explain to her that the heart of the gospel is that Jesus wants that rose.

Filled with compassion, Jesus let the woman standing in front of him know she was not defined by her sin. She wasn't the worst thing she'd ever done. She wasn't worthless because of what she had done. Her worth was based on God's love for her.

If she was defined by her sin, it would make sin the ultimate power and authority. But *God* is the ultimate power and authority, and she was defined by his love. All of that became a reality to her because Jesus showed her compassion instead of condemnation.

Jesus changed everything and, when he did, I think the worst day of her life became her best day.

A New Command

Look again at what Jesus said in John 13:34: "A new command I give you: Love one another. As I have loved you, so you must love one another."

We are to love others as Jesus loved us. One of the primary ways Jesus loves us one at a time is by forgiving us when we don't deserve it. That's how we are to love others one at a time. We are to "be kind and compassionate to one another, forgiving each other, just as in Christ God forgave you" (Eph. 4:32).

One more Scripture:

> Whoever says, "I know him," but does not do what he commands is a liar, and the truth is not in that person. But if anyone obeys his word, love for God is truly made complete in them. This is how we know we are in him: Whoever claims to live in him must live as Jesus did. . . . Anyone who claims to be in the light but hates a brother or sister is still in the darkness. Anyone who loves their brother and sister lives in the light. (1 John 2:4–6, 9–10)

I know a guy who is tempted to skip over or skim through the Bible verses quoted in books he reads because he thinks he already knows the Bible.*

Can I encourage you to go back and read that last passage again?

If we know Jesus and want to know we are in him, we must live and love as Jesus did. That means offering forgiveness and grace.†

I love the way 1 Corinthians 13 describes this kind of Jesus love. It's a love that "keeps no record of wrongs" (v. 5). When faced with a sinner, a blasphemer, a betrayer, an accuser, a denier, Jesus demonstrated compassion and grace.

Is that how you love?

---

*I may be that guy.
†That's a recap of 1 John 2, because I know you didn't go back and reread it. We're so much alike.

My assumption is that most Christians would give a vigorous yes to that question. But I also know that Christians today are *not* known for compassion and grace. Something doesn't add up.

I think part of the confusion is we consider ourselves to love that way in general, but we are often not acting it out *specifically*. Meaning that we agree with grace and compassion theoretically, but we have a hard time putting it into practice with people one at a time. I think there are some reasons for that.

Grace Challenge #1: Not Recognizing Our Own Sin

We have trouble thinking of ourselves as sinners. I mean, we know we're not perfect but, well, it just seems like other people's sins are a lot worse.

We rationalize or just don't recognize our sin, which makes us feel superior to others. That spirit of feeling *better than* can lead us to a place of condemnation instead of compassion.

That is . . . exactly the opposite of Jesus.

Think about this: God says if you're guilty of sin, you can't judge the sin of someone else. Only Jesus had no sin. So only Jesus had the right to judge. When the men dragged the woman in front of Jesus and wanted to stone her, Jesus said, "If you have no sin, you can condemn her. You can give her what she deserves."

Go back to the teaching from the Sermon on the Mount in Matthew 5. After Jesus put angry people in the same circle as murderers, he put people who lust in the same circle as those who have committed adultery.

You have heard that it was said, "You shall not commit adultery." But I tell you that anyone who looks at a woman lustfully has already committed adultery with her in his heart. (v. 27)

Jesus is speaking to those who believe they're better than people who commit adultery. You might think adultery is someone else's sin, but adultery is your sin too. I wonder if Jesus wrote only one word in the dirt that day: *lust*.

These religious leaders didn't have the love or compassion Jesus did for her because they didn't see their sins were just as offensive to God—even if their sins couldn't be seen by others.

C. S. Lewis talked about this in his book *Mere Christianity*. Specifically, he spoke of his annoyance with the perception of many that sexual sin is somehow the worst of all sins. He wrote,

> The sins of the flesh are bad, but they are the least bad of all sins. All the worst pleasures are purely spiritual: the pleasure of putting other people in the wrong, of bossing and patronizing and spoiling sport, and back-biting; the pleasures of power, of hatred. For there are two things inside me . . . they are the Animal self, and the Diabolical self. The Diabolical self is the worse of the two. That is why a cold, self-righteous prig who goes regularly to church may be far nearer to hell than a prostitute. But, of course, it is better to be neither.[3]

Don't be an angry, self-righteous prig—recognize your sinfulness.

Jesus helped the religious leaders realize they were in no position to judge this woman in self-righteous anger, and so they dropped their stones and walked.

Jesus, on the other hand, had every right to judge her but didn't. He said, "Then neither do I condemn you. . . . Go now and leave your life of sin" (John 8:11).

Jesus used his position of sinlessness not to condemn but to offer grace. Speaking the truth to her about no longer living in sin did not require condemnation. The verse after the Bible's most famous verse tells us, "God did not send his Son into the world to condemn the world, but to save the world through him" (John 3:17).

We need to recognize our sin and realize we're in no place to judge. In the words of C. S. Lewis, don't be a prig.

And if you somehow reach a place of near sinlessness, you can love like Jesus did by using that position to offer grace and kindness.

Grace Challenge #2: Compassion without Condoning

Some Christians may be hesitant to offer this kind of grace because they're afraid people will mistake it for an acceptance of sin, or even a license to continue sinning. They conclude that they can't really show people love until the person stops sinning, otherwise people may think what they did or what they're doing is no big deal. The concern is that their compassion will be confused as condoning.

That, however, is the opposite of what Jesus did and commands us to do. Remember Romans 5:8–10? "But God demonstrates his own love for us in this: While we were still sinners . . ."

We choose compassion based on the unconditional love of God and trust in the saving power of Jesus and the sanctifying work of the Holy Spirit.

Compassion doesn't equal condoning.

If you show someone compassion and they confuse that as condoning, that is a mistake on their part because the two are *not* the same. Jesus did not condemn the woman but did tell her to go and sin no more.

We aren't telling people, "God loves you just the way you are, so keep doing what you're doing." I've heard the message of God's love summed up this way: "God loves you just the way you are, but he loves you too much to leave you that way."

Accepting a sinner is *not* accepting their sin, but some people probably will take it that way. And? I think it's worth the risk. How do I know that? Because it is a risk God is willing to take.

God's grace is so amazing, so outlandish, that some people *do* mistake it for an acceptance of sin. That's the way it has always been. If you read Romans 6, you will see that it was happening two thousand years ago. This is not an excuse to withhold compassion and grace from someone in your life.

Philip Yancey said, "While every other religion offers a way to earn approval, only Christianity dares to make God's love unconditional."[4]

If God is willing to offer a grace so amazing, even knowing that some *will* mistake it for acceptance of or license to sin, shouldn't we also be willing to take that risk?

We hope people don't make that mistake, but we offer unconditional love regardless.

The challenge is to not just accept that theoretically but to offer that to people in your life one at a time.

The Rest of Caleb's Story

My friend Caleb went to a Bible study to return some of the hate he had experienced from Christians at the gay pride parades. But the Christians he met in that Bible study gave him a very different impression of Jesus.

Caleb started reading the Bible, and everything changed for him when he read John 8. He saw how Jesus chose compassion when confronted with a woman caught in sin and a crowd who wanted to condemn her. *This* was the real Jesus, not the picture the angry, screaming Christians had given him at the rallies.

Caleb put his faith in and surrendered his entire life to Jesus.

He was sixteen.

His mother disowned him. His father asked him to move out.

He moved in with Joe, the guy who led the Bible study he had been attending.

A couple years later, Caleb went to seminary, where he and I became friends. That was back in the 1990s. Check this out: a few years ago, Caleb baptized his mother and father, who had both put their faith in Jesus.

How did that happen?

They learned through the people they met at the church Caleb pastored that not all Christians are like the prigs they'd been exposed to. They met Christians who chose compassion instead of condemnation. They met the real, loving Jesus. The Jesus who does not let our sins define us but provides a path out of them and into freedom.

That Jesus, the *real* Jesus, is really irresistible. So they gave their lives to Jesus, and Jesus changed their lives.

It happened because a guy named Joe and the kids in the Bible study group loved one at a time.

PART 2

living
one
at a time

one party
at a time

QUICK, WHAT DOES GOD have in common with the Beastie Boys?*

Back in 1986, the Beastie Boys told everyone to fight for their right to party. Seemed a little intense, but I guess they were really into partying.

Back in Leviticus 23, God told everyone to party or he would kill them. That's very intense, but I guess God is really into partying.

Both God and the Beastie Boys believe that partying is a right and a responsibility.

I know you're skeptical but stick with me.

In the Old Testament, God set up a series of annual parties for his people. These elaborate festivals were designed to be commemorative and anticipatory. God's people were

---

*I just googled that question and apparently no one has ever asked it before.

to come together to celebrate what he had done *and* what he would do.

God wanted his people to practice gratitude and live with expectancy. To recognize God's fingerprints all over the blessings they had received and to have the faith to live with a joyful anticipation of what he might do next. God didn't want them to just live that way, he wanted them to come together and *party* with that purpose.

That's the Old Testament.

In the New Testament, Jesus shows up and fights for his right to party. We repeatedly see Jesus at parties. So much so, it led to an accusation the religious leaders made against him: "Here is a glutton and a drunkard, a friend of tax collectors and sinners" (Matt. 11:19).

Jesus also compared God's kingdom to a party and, in a famous trilogy of stories, taught that when someone turns to God, a party breaks out in heaven (Luke 15).

Don't miss this: in the Bible, there's a clear and consistent party theology. Missiologist* Alan Hirsh says, "Party is sacrament."[1] Sacraments are the significant, long-held practices or ceremonies that set the church apart and hold the church together. Sacraments include baptism, taking the Lord's Supper, marriage, and . . . *partying*? If you google "Christian sacraments," you won't find partying on any list, but maybe that's a problem.

Could it be we have lost something vital God wants for his people?

---

*A missiologist is not someone who is always missing things. Actually, it's someone who studies the mission God gave his people in the Bible and how it's accomplished today through various forms of missionary activity.

It reminds me of something I experienced a couple years ago after a church service. A man came up and informed me, "I think somebody should say something to the young man who walked forward wearing a baseball cap. It's really not appropriate to wear that baseball cap in church."

I examined his face to make sure he wasn't joking. He wasn't.

I said, "Oh, you mean the young man who didn't grow up in church but walked forward to give his life to Christ and be baptized? You want me to say something to him about the baseball cap he was wearing?"

He apparently wasn't fluent in sarcasm because he responded, "Yeah! Somebody should say something to him."

My adrenaline increased and hit a place where I knew I needed to walk away and find a later opportunity to correct his thinking.

Maybe in a book or something.

I think that upset man represents so many Christians who have lost the celebratory spirit that led God to require partying in the Old Testament and Jesus to repeatedly go to and talk about parties in the New Testament.

Party-*less* Christians today may represent the Pharisees in Jesus's day, who lost the heart of God and made their faith about keeping rules and traditions. Jesus showed up to destroy what the Pharisees had made of religion. He came and brought partying back.

It turns out that throwing a party is one of the best ways to influence and value people one at a time.

Why?

Parties Bring Joy

Let's say someone asked you to describe *God's will*. What would you say? Perhaps "Always be joyful. Never stop praying. Be thankful in all circumstances, for this is God's will for you who belong to Christ Jesus" (1 Thess. 5:16–18 NLT)?

This might not be what you expect, but God tells us his will includes *joy*. Always.

When the angels announced the birth of Jesus, their message was, "Do not be afraid. I bring you good news that will cause great joy for all the people" (Luke 2:10).

Jesus came to bring *great joy*.

Jesus came to bring his joy and *fill us with it*. He said, "These things I have spoken to you, that my joy may be in you, and that your joy may be full" (John 15:11 ESV).

God's will, the Good News of Jesus, is about joy. Yet listen to how someone once described their perception of Christianity: "Christianity is the haunting fear that someone somewhere is having a good time."

That is the perception a *lot* of people have of Christianity. We've got to put a stop to that.

We need to give people a different view of who Jesus is by giving them a different view of who we are as his followers. Not only because a joyless Christianity misrepresents Jesus and the will of God but also because a joyless Christianity is unattractive.

Jesus didn't draw crowds to himself and impact people one at a time by being joyless. People were drawn to him and will be to us because of *joy*.

Joy is attractive, and parties bring joy.

Parties Bring the Kingdom

Let's say someone asked you to describe *God's kingdom*. What would you say? Perhaps "For the kingdom of God is not a matter of eating and drinking, but of righteousness, peace and joy" (Rom. 14:17)?

This might not be what you expect, but God tells us his kingdom is about *joy*. Jesus said we are to seek God's kingdom *and* bring it to earth (see Matt. 6:10, 33). That means we are to be seekers of joy and bringers of joy.

Jesus compared the kingdom of God to a party—see Matthew 22:1–14, for example—and if we are going to bring the kingdom of God to earth, we need to throw some parties. We live in a "post-Christian" and "cancel" culture that is increasingly rejecting the church and ostracizing Christians, but people are always ready for a good party.

I mentioned missiologists, people who study the mission God has given us and how we can most effectively accomplish it. Here's something my friend Hugh Halter, another one of those missiologists, said to me: "When asked about the one true key to bringing people far from God near, I simply say, 'Start throwing great parties.'"

I believe that. We can love people one at a time by throwing parties.

In fact, one year our church made it an emphasis. We asked our people to throw parties in a way that would allow them to love and serve others in Jesus's name, and help those who had rejected Jesus to get a new view of him and his followers.

We explained that parties with a purpose can create and grow relationships, and relationships are how we love like Jesus and point people to him.

Accept Invitations to Parties

Jesus was invited to parties.

It says something that people wanted him at their parties. For instance, in John 2 we read of a wedding party and we're told, "Jesus and his disciples had also been invited to the wedding" (v. 2).

Doesn't that seem a little weird? If you didn't know anything about Jesus or the Bible, and someone told you that God came to earth and lived a human life, would you expect this God-human to be invited to parties?

I might guess that people would be like, "Don't invite the God-human. He'll be walking around with his good/bad checklist on a clipboard, spying around corners, shaking his head in disapproving ways. It's a hard *no* to inviting the God-human."

But that's not what happened. Jesus was invited to parties. Someone making their list of who was wanted at the party said, "Oh! We definitely need to invite Jesus. He's a lot of fun. People love him!"

Question: Are you invited to parties? Do the people who know you—in your neighborhood or at work—want you around because you're positive and fun and encouraging? Or do you not get the invite because people assume you'd stand in a corner giving everyone a disapproving stink eye?

Jesus was invited to parties, and *he accepted the invitations.*

Again, this is a bit surprising to me. I would assume Jesus wouldn't have the time. Wedding parties back then were weeklong events. Jesus knew his time was limited. He had a lot to accomplish.

I can picture his administrative assistant saying, "Well, looks like you have to write your 'Sermon on the Mount'—by the way, are you still sure that's the best name for it? No disrespect, but I just can't picture that going viral. What about 'How to Be Happy' or something a little more catchy? Anyway, you have to write that, and there's your leadership pipeline. You've got these junior executives you've chosen who, frankly, need a *lot* of training. Also, you've got to perform at least a few miracles sometime soon. We need to create some momentum. So, weeklong wedding party? Sorry, no can do. That's not going to happen."

Jesus came to change the world, but his time on earth was relatively short. His ministry lasted little more than a few years, and yet he accepted invitations to weeklong parties. He made time to have fun with other people.

Do you accept invitations to parties? Too often Christians can stay in the comfort of their Christian bubble, avoiding social situations that might be awkward.

I get it. I'll choose comfortable over awkward every time. But that's not the choice Jesus made, and I choose to follow Jesus.

Bring Joy to the Party

Jesus was invited to parties, accepted the invitation, and *brought joy to the party*.

On the third day of the weeklong wedding party in John 2, they ran out of wine. That doesn't sound like that big of a deal. When we ran out of chicken wings at our Super Bowl party, I just ordered pizza.

But in the first-century culture, it was a *big* deal to run out of wine at a wedding. In Jewish culture, wine was a symbol of joy. There was a rabbinic saying at the time, "There is no rejoicing without wine." The idea was based on Old Testament Scriptures like Psalm 104:15, "God made wine to bring joy to the human heart" (my paraphrase). Running out of wine was symbolic of running out of joy. Not a great omen for the newlyweds.

In their eyes, they no longer had joy. But they *did* have Jesus. So Mary, Jesus's mother, goes to him, tells him what the problem is, and instructs the servants working the wedding, "Do whatever he tells you" (John 2:5).

Jesus tells the servers to fill six stone water jars—each able to hold twenty to thirty gallons—with water and then take some out and give it to the host of the party. They do it, and the host drinks what was water but is now wine and proclaims that it's the best he's had.

I love that Jesus brought joy—about 150 gallons of it!—to the party.

Jesus's *followers* need to bring joy.

When I was a pastor in California, I officiated a beautiful wedding at an elegant hotel in Los Angeles. I didn't know many people there, but I was good friends with a groomsman, and I thought staying for the party was a perk of doing the wedding.

After dinner, the DJ was trying to get some energy in the room, but it really wasn't happening. I was watching with curiosity when I started to feel self-conscious, like people were looking at me. My buddy, the groomsman, came over and asked, "Yo, Kyle, what are your plans for tonight?"

I was confused. "Well, I was, you know, planning on staying here at the party."

He smiled. "So Kyle, hey, this is kind of funny, but, well, I think a lot of people are waiting for you to leave so the party can actually start."

Ohhhhh, I get it.

Apparently, their personal experience had led them to think that they couldn't party with a pastor, but that is *not* the effect I want to have on parties.

Jesus brought joy to parties, and so should we.

Turning water into wine at the wedding party was Jesus's first miracle. Sometimes when people teach on this passage, they make it sound like the reason Jesus did it was because his mother told him to. Mom said, "Jesus, they're out of wine, do something!" and Jesus was like, "Oh man. Mommmmm! Really? I wanted to make my first miracle something more dramatic. This isn't very cool. I mean, wine is already 86 percent water. Really, I'd only be changing 14 percent of it. What if I at least turned water into chicken wings? Whatever. I'll turn water into wine, but only because you're my mom."

I doubt it. The angels announced Jesus was coming to bring great joy, and he began his ministry by bringing joy to a wedding party. I don't think that was an accident. In Revelation we read about heaven as a great wedding banquet where our joy will be made complete.

And I love how Jesus's first miracle would've been such a tangible expression to *one* person: the bride. Running out of wine may not seem like a big deal to you, but I promise it was a big deal to her. With his first miracle, Jesus modeled the one at a time approach to life.

Jesus brought joy. Jesus's followers bring joy. One of the ways we do that is by accepting invitations to parties.

Extend Invitations to Parties

Jesus's followers don't just dutifully go to parties when invited, they *throw parties*. In Luke 5, Jesus was walking along when he "saw a tax collector by the name of Levi sitting at his tax booth. 'Follow me,' Jesus said to him, and Levi got up, left everything and followed him" (vv. 27–28).

Levi, or Matthew as he would more often be called, was a tax collector, which meant he was at the top of everyone's most-despised list. Tax collectors were Jews who sided with the occupying and oppressive Roman government. They would collect taxes from the Jews to give to the Romans. Like mafiosos, tax collectors would strong-arm the locals into giving them extra money, which they would put in their own pockets.

Levi was hated, avoided, and declared unclean. The religious leaders wouldn't allow him into the temple. Yet Jesus came along and invited Levi to be his disciple. Levi left everything to follow Jesus.

If you're Levi, what do you do next?

"Then Levi held a great banquet for Jesus at his house, and a large crowd of tax collectors and others were eating with them" (v. 29).

As a follower of Jesus, the most natural thing for Levi was to throw a party. He invited a bunch of his friends who were far from God, and he invited Jesus. It was the perfect opportunity for his friends to get a real picture of who Jesus really was.

The Pharisees were aghast and demanded that Jesus answer their accusing question: "Why do you eat and drink with tax collectors and sinners?" (v. 30).

They didn't understand why Jesus was at a party, especially at a party with those people. Jesus answered, "It is not the healthy who need a doctor, but the sick. I have not come to call the righteous, but sinners to repentance" (vv. 31–32). *C'mon, you don't get it? That's why I've come. That's why my followers throw parties, and that's why the invitation list is filled with people who are far from God.*

I love that. Jesus is basically saying, "Of course parties, of course sinners. What did you expect?"

Throwing a party might be one of the most natural things a Christ-follower can do. It might be one of the most *spiritual* things a Christ-follower can do.

So, what if *you* threw a party?

What kind of party? A party with a purpose. A party that points people to Jesus. A party that brings joy to people one at a time.

Oikos Parties

One type of party you can throw is an *oikos* party. Oikos isn't the Greek word for *yogurt*; it's actually the Greek word for *home* or *household*, but it's sometimes also used for people who are close to you, like your family and more intimate friends.

So, an oikos party would be one where you invite people in your relational network—it might be coworkers, classmates, neighbors, the guys in your fantasy football league, the moms from your kid's swim lesson group. Levi's bash is a great example of an oikos party.

The thinking behind an oikos party is to *relationally engage people who are spiritually unengaged.*

Remember how Jesus's mother told the servers, "Do whatever he tells you"? That's a great philosophy of life, and Jesus has told us to seek and save the lost. He gave us a mission of making disciples of people who don't believe, to baptize them and teach them to obey Jesus's commands. We are to pursue people who have pulled away from God.

One way to do that is with a party.

Please note: evangelism doesn't need to happen *at* the party. I'm not suggesting you do the bait-and-switch Super Bowl party where you invite people to watch the game but then pause it to share a testimony, and everyone leaves a little bitter.

Think of this oikos party more like *pre*-evangelism. Use the party to deepen connections and build relationships, believing that it will lead to opportunities to share your faith. It's building a bridge so at a later time you can cross over it and talk to them about Jesus.

When we asked people in our church to throw parties, one elementary school principal decided to surprise his teachers. He told them they'd be having an all-day training and that they could dress casually.

In the morning, there was training, and when it was time to break for lunch, the principal called to the stage a lady from our church who volunteered at the school. This woman shared with the teachers why she loved volunteering *and* that she loved to party—and she'd brought some of her friends from church who were also into partying. The teachers then walked to the cafeteria to find balloons and a line of volunteers waiting to serve them. They got their food and walked outside, where they heard music blasting and saw a seventy-foot inflatable obstacle course and all kinds of games. The volunteers put on some fun competitions and gave out great prizes.

It was an amazing afternoon, and the teachers kept asking the volunteers from our church, "Why?" They smiled and answered, "Because we love teachers."

Evangelism may not have happened at that party, but pre-evangelism *definitely* did. Those volunteers from the church gave the teachers a different view of who Jesus is by giving them a different view of who we are as his followers. By throwing a party, they brought joy.

In Luke 15, Jesus tells us to pursue people who have pulled away from God, and that when one comes back to him, a great party breaks out in heaven.

I can't wait to hear about the parties that happen in heaven because of the party that was thrown at Blue Lick Elementary School.

Xenos Parties

A second type of party you might throw is a *xenos* party. Xenos is the Greek word for *stranger* or *foreigner*. God tells us in Hebrews 13:2, "Do not forget to show hospitality to strangers."

"Strangers" comes from that Greek word xenos, but the original Greek verse actually uses a compound word, *philoxenias*, that has been translated into English as "show hospitality to strangers" but has a more literal translation of "love strangers." We have been commanded to love strangers, and one of the best ways we can do so is by throwing parties and inviting them.

In Luke 14 we see Jesus at yet another party. This party was thrown by a religious leader, and the invite list was composed of religious leaders. Typically a pretty lame party—but not when Jesus showed up.

At the party, people networked and vied for recognition and the most honorable seats at the table. Jesus was not impressed. He challenged them, "Why don't you guys invite someone who *can't* do something for you? What if you invited the overlooked and undervalued? How about inviting the kind of people who never get invited?" (see vv. 12–14).

The thinking that drives a xenos party is that *Jesus engaged those whom other people avoided*. It's connecting with people who are unconnected. As Jesus's followers, we need to find surprising ways to serve those who otherwise might be shunned, so . . . how about a party?

One of the parties our church members threw was at Parliament Square, which are partially Section 8 apartments that are home to some of the lowest-income families in Louisville. A bunch of Jesus people got together and threw a Jesus party for the kids of Parliament Square. They called it a back-to-school party and provided the kids with great food and all the school supplies they needed. These kids, who so often went unnoticed, were served and celebrated.

Another party our church threw was for single moms. We invited single moms to come to a class with childcare provided, but after they dropped off their kids they were led to a bus that took them all to a surprise night out to make them feel special and loved on.

We also threw a party for refugees. As you might imagine, settling in a new country is challenging, and the first three months can be especially difficult. We invited folks who had recently settled in Louisville to a party, and 250 showed up! Of those 250 people, there were twelve different nations represented.

I have to believe heaven celebrates when we celebrate people created in God's image but who too often are denied the dignity they deserve.

Your Party

I bet God is calling you to throw a party, and I wonder what type of party it is. The idea of it might freak you out a little. I understand. I am not, by nature, a thrower of parties. But good news: it's something that can be *learned*.

Hugh Halter, that party-loving missiologist I mentioned earlier, also told me, "You have to teach and disciple people in how to throw a good party."

It's not as difficult as you think. Here are a few ideas: greet people at the door. Show that you are happy to see them. Smile! Turn on all your lights—darkness does not communicate joy. Put on some upbeat music, and extra points if it's songs your guests already know and probably like. Offer food. It doesn't have to be fancy but save the stale half-bag of potato chips for yourself. Think of something fun you could do together, like play a board game, watch a funny video, or play pin-the-tail-on-your-husband.

Not all parties are the same, and I would encourage you to let your personality and passions guide you. Perhaps yours could be

a block party cookout for your neighborhood.

you and your friends playing video games together.

a surprise appreciation party for the firefighters at your local station.

getting together with some guys for a *Hot Ones*–style time of eating insanely hot wings and asking each other interview questions.

a "watch the big finale of your favorite show" get-together.

a pool party for everyone on your kid's team.

a fancy dinner because you're a foodie who loves to cook.

The possibilities are endless, and you can uniquely design your party based on the unique way God designed you.

Nice to Be Noticed

Some of the people in our church threw a party in a parking lot. Maybe this doesn't seem like the best ambiance for a party, but it's a lot where people park their cars and then get on a bus that takes them to their workplace in the city. People park in this lot early in the morning, so instead of hors d'oeuvres the party refreshments were muffins and juice. The party throwers cranked music and put out games people could play as they waited for the bus.

One woman who was walking toward the bus from her car was obviously distressed. A few volunteers asked if they could give her some snacks for the road.

She declined, then stopped and asked, "Are you from a church?"

When they said yes, she asked, "Would you . . . would you please pray for my family? We just found out last night that my daughter is addicted to heroin."

She rushed off and got on her bus, and then looked out the window and saw people she didn't know who were now huddled together praying for her daughter.

Wow.

There was another person who was walking toward the bus but stopped for some juice and a muffin. She started to leave, then paused and said, "Hey, thanks for doing this. Sometimes it's nice just to be noticed."

That's the heart of heaven.

When one person at a time is noticed, valued, loved, pursued, and ultimately rescued, that's what leads heaven to throw a party—and it often happens because *we* threw a party.

one word
at a time

IT'S TIME FOR ME to tell you about Ignaz Semmelweis.
Yeah, I know. You've been waiting.

Dr. Ignaz Semmelweis worked at two maternity clinics in the 1840s. The clinics were right next to each other. One was staffed by doctors and the other by midwives.

Inspecting the results at each clinic, Dr. Semmelweis noticed at the one run by doctors, women were dying of childbed fever at a five times greater rate than at the midwife clinic. That was, obviously, unacceptable.

He started investigating what each clinic was doing differently. He eventually realized the doctors, unlike the midwives, would do autopsies of the women who died and then immediately go deliver a baby without washing their hands or instruments.

It's obvious to us that this would be a problem, but it wasn't back then. Years later Louis Pasteur would discover germs, but in the 1840s people had no idea. Semmelweis didn't know *why* it would make any difference, but even still he told the doctors, "Let's wash our hands and our instruments. We'll use chlorine."

He didn't know chlorine was a disinfectant. He just thought it would get rid of the smell from the corpses. He wondered if maybe the smell was part of the problem.*

The doctors at the clinic started washing their hands and instruments and, of course, it changed everything. They realized—even though they didn't understand why and it seemed insignificant—that washing their hands was a matter of life and death.

I think we can relate.

We inspect our lives and notice some things that are unacceptable. We decide we want to change everything. We try, but after some failed results we stop trying.

What if the secret to impacting one person at a time is something that seems insignificant? Would you be willing to try it even if you don't understand why it works?

Really?

Okay then, here it is: *words.*

Your words have the power of life and death.

Seem a bit overstated?

I might agree, except it's what God tells us. One word at a time to one person at a time, "The tongue has the power of life and death" (Prov. 18:21).

---

*It was 1840; give the guy a break. Society had not yet even figured out the technology to stuff yellow sponge cake with cream filling and make a Twinkie.

We speak around sixteen thousand words per day. Granted, some of you are skewing that number big-time. But on average we each speak sixteen thousand words every day. I wonder if the sheer number of words we speak makes it easy to underestimate the significance that each word can have. Sixteen thousand words a day is like writing a sixty-page book every day with the words you speak. And each of those words matters.

So much of loving and impacting people the way Jesus did is about the words we speak. In fact, words create worlds.

Are Words Worthless?

Like the doctors who couldn't understand why their pal Ignaz was making such a big deal about washing hands, you might think words are not that significant.

I get it. I don't think of words as being so weighty, except when I get called out because of my word choices.

One time I was speaking at my church about how we have a tendency to just want to lie around and do nothing. I decided to describe our laziness with a phrase I had seen on social media. I said, "Sometimes we just want to Netflix and chill." I thought I was hip for using a phrase that was popular with the younger crowd. Until I walked off the stage and saw my phone was blowing up.

I received numerous texts warning me, "I don't think that means what you think it means!"

Someone asked me, "Kyle, what do you think it means?" I answered, "It means to watch TV and relax."

I was then encouraged to look up what it actually means. I did. It *actually* means to watch TV and . . . well . . . it turns out "Netflix and chill" is a euphemism for sex.* But I was just trying to be cool. I had no idea what those words meant.

I think maybe that's our problem. We're careless about the words we speak because we're naïve to their power.

Words Create Worlds

God created the world with the power of his words. He literally spoke the world into existence. We're told in Genesis 1 that there was just nothingness, but God *spoke* into it: "And God said, 'Let there be light,' and there was light" (v. 3). God said it and it was. Soon there was a galaxy with an earth filled with water and plants and people. God spoke the universe into existence. From the beginning, words had the power of life.

Flip a couple pages in the Bible, and we see that words have the power of death too. In Genesis 3, sin entered the world. Satan came on the scene in the form of a serpent and got Adam and Eve to rebel against God.

How did he do it? He spoke. Satan used words to bring death where there was life and darkness where there was light.

What's interesting is that the serpent's words weren't true but that didn't keep them from having power. God hardwired the power of words into the universe.

---

*Euphemisms for sex can be hard to keep up with. One from the 1800s was "basket making." As in, "Hey, honey, are you interested in some basket making?"

If we turn to the New Testament, we find John introducing Jesus as "the Word."

> In the beginning was the Word, and the Word was with God, and the Word was God. He was with God in the beginning. Through him all things were made; without him nothing was made that has been made. In him was life, and that life was the light of all mankind. The light shines in the darkness, and the darkness has not overcome it. (John 1:1–5)

Remember how, in Genesis 1, God spoke light into the darkness? In John 1 we learn that Jesus is the Word God spoke. He is the Word in human flesh.

Throughout his ministry, we see Jesus using words to bring heaven to earth. He tells his disciples he must go *speak* to people because "that is why I have come" (Mark 1:38).

Jesus begins the first recorded teaching we have of his by saying, "The Spirit of the Lord is on me, because he has anointed me to proclaim" (Luke 4:18).

Jesus came to proclaim, to speak.

Of course he did, because words create worlds.

Jesus constantly used words to speak life and healing and blessing. When in a boat with a raging storm, what did he do? He rebuked the storm. He spoke to it. He didn't just think the thought, wrinkle his nose like the gal in *Bewitched*, or do a "Quit it, now" gesture with his hands.*

*You know, that one your dad used to do at you when you were fighting with your sibling in the back seat of the car.

He said, "Peace! Be still!" and the moment he spoke, the storm became calm (Mark 4:39 ESV). There was power in his words.

Jesus arrived at the tomb of his friend Lazarus and raised him from death to life. How? Did he go into the tomb and slap Lazarus on the forehead like some faith healer you might see on TV? Nope.

Did he dramatically remove the stone from the tomb like a Las Vegas magician, revealing Lazarus was alive again? Nope.

What did Jesus do? He spoke. He called, "Lazarus, come out!" and Lazarus came out (John 11:43–44).

If we want to live and love like Jesus, we need to understand that words have the power of life and death and start choosing them carefully.

A Dinner Party and Some Detective Work

One of my favorite one at a time stories is found in Luke 7. Jesus was invited to a dinner party by a Pharisee named Simon. The Pharisees were the religious leaders of the time, and they were all about rules designed to ensure purity.† In fact, before dinner, everyone would have gone through a ritualistic cleansing, as they did before every meal, making sure they were purified from anything that might have defiled them from their time out in the world that day.

Something completely unexpected happened in the middle of this dinner party that broke all their rules.

†Picture a combination of the Soup Nazi from *Seinfeld* and the DMV worker you have nightmares about, and you're imagining a Pharisee.

"A woman in that town who lived a sinful life learned that Jesus was eating at the Pharisee's house, so she came there with an alabaster jar of perfume" (v. 37).

The words "a woman who had lived a sinful life" was code for "the town prostitute."

She heard Jesus was eating at the Pharisee's house, showed up uninvited, and burst through the door. She represented everything the Pharisees were against and, from the Pharisees' perspective, this despised woman entering the room would have destroyed the ritual purity they had established for the evening.

She would have known how they viewed her, that she was persona non grata. It didn't matter. She couldn't help herself.

"As she stood behind him at his feet weeping, she began to wet his feet with her tears. Then she wiped them with her hair, kissed them and poured perfume on them" (v. 38).

She walked into the room and knew how people were looking at her. But she saw Jesus, and no man had ever looked at her the way he did. She was undone by his love and grace.

She didn't know what to say—or perhaps she knew but couldn't get the words out once she was actually there. She just fell at his feet. Her tears cascaded off her cheeks and onto Jesus's feet, so she let down her hair to dry them.

There must have been an audible gasp in the room. She was breaking all the rules. Women didn't let down their hair in that culture. It was considered scandalous. In fact, a woman letting her hair down in front of a man who was not her husband was considered such an intimate expression it was grounds for divorce.

She didn't care. She let her hair down and dried Jesus's feet.

Everyone was expecting him to rebuke her, to say something like, "Woman, what are you doing? Don't you know how inappropriate this is?"

He didn't.

She had with her an alabaster jar of perfume. The perfume was worth a *lot*. It was the equivalent of about a year's wages. She took it, broke it open, and poured all of its contents on Jesus.

This jar represented the life she had lived and what she had put her trust in. She was giving it all up because she had a new life and something else to put her trust in. Her focus was now on Jesus, and she didn't care about the perfume, her savings, or what anyone in the room thought of her.

Everyone was shocked by her display. We're told the host Pharisee assumed Jesus must not realize what kind of sinner this woman was. In response, Jesus told a story and then proclaimed that this woman did what she did because she was forgiven much (see v. 47). Then he turned to her and said, "Your faith has saved you; go in peace" (v. 50).

Wow! I love that story, and I wonder, what led her to surrender her life to and worship Jesus with such abandon?

I need to know because *I* want to impact people like that. We want to impact people so they come to believe in and love Jesus in such an overwhelming way that they give it all. But how?

Well, Jesus said she couldn't help but express her gratitude because she had been forgiven much.

Apparently this woman, maybe earlier that day or the day before, had heard Jesus speak his message of love and forgiveness. It must have been hearing Jesus's words that changed her, but what did she hear him say?

Luke, who shares this story, doesn't tell us what Jesus said that day. But with a little detective work, we might be able to figure it out. Earlier in this chapter, we're told that some disciples of John the Baptist had shown up to ask Jesus whether he really was the Messiah. In Matthew 11, one of the other Gospels, we also read about this incident with John the Baptist's disciples, so we know it's the same day, and Matthew *does* tell us what Jesus taught that day.

Imagine this woman, the town prostitute, standing in the back of the crowd, looking at Jesus and listening to Jesus, this man who claimed to represent God, a man who was obviously so different from any man she had ever met. Then he *speaks*, and his words have power. Here's what Jesus said that day:

Come to me, all you who are weary and burdened, and I will give you rest. Take my yoke upon you and learn from me, for I am gentle and humble in heart, and you will find rest for your souls. (Matt. 11:28–29)

Can you imagine how that sounded to her?

Who knows how she had gotten where she was, or what had happened in her life. The vast majority of women in the sex industry today were abused as children, often sexually abused. Maybe that was her story. I don't know. But I do know she had grown up into a life filled with words of condemnation. Being condemned by others and, I would assume, condemning herself.

She didn't grow up hoping to become a prostitute. No little girl dreams of that. No one grows up planning on being ashamed of their sin. They just end up there.

She thought "there" was where she would always stay. How could she escape her life and start over? Who could help her out of this life? The only response she received from anyone was condemnation, and that didn't change her. Pointing out her sins didn't lead her out of them. Shame didn't set her free. She thought this would always be her life.

But here's Jesus, God come down from heaven, saying the words, "Come to me. Find rest for your soul."

In that moment she realized it didn't matter who she was, what she had done, or what anyone else thought of her. *God* was for her and was offering forgiveness, relationship, freedom, and new life.

The only way to respond to Jesus's words was with the word *yes*.

Later, she heard Jesus was a dinner guest at Simon the Pharisee's house, so she grabbed her most valued treasure and headed over.

She walked in, and this broken woman fell at Jesus's feet and broke her jar.

Jesus explained to Simon that the reason she did it was because of gratitude, because she had been forgiven much. And, to make sure no one missed the point, Jesus turned to the woman, and spoke a few more lifegiving words. "Your sins are forgiven. . . . Your faith has saved you; go in peace" (Luke 7:48, 50).

She walked out that day with a whole new life. Jesus's words had created a new world for her.

Jesus forgave her sins, which is something we can't do.

But God *has* given us the power to speak words of life, and our words create worlds.

Your World

Your world was created by the power of words.

You've had people who spoke lifegiving words to you, who helped you believe in God, in yourself, in the possibility of change. Those words built you up and created the positive things you appreciate about your life today.

You've also probably had some words spoken to you that felt like death and have stayed with you ever since. I asked my Facebook friends to give examples of words that were tattooed on their souls and shaped their lives in a negative way. Within minutes I received responses like, "No one will ever want to be with you," "You're damaged goods," "You are irresponsible," "You're just not smart enough," "I wish you were never born," "I'm just not attracted to you anymore," "You lost the game for us tonight," and "Why can't you be more like your sister?"

Matthew Lieberman, a neuroscientist, noticed we tend to use the language of physical pain to talk about relational pain. We say things like, "She *broke* my heart," "He *hurt* my feelings," and "Those words were a *punch* in the gut." Lieberman decided to study the difference in the brain when we experience physical pain versus relational pain. His conclusion? In his book *Social: Why Our Brains Are Wired to Connect*, Lieberman wrote, "Looking at the brain scans side by side, without knowing which was an analysis of physical pain and which was an analysis of social pain, you wouldn't have been able to tell the difference."[1]

Remember that old saying, "Sticks and stones may break my bones, but words will never hurt me"? It's not true. Emotional pain is just as real and just as painful as physical pain.

It reminds me of when I came back from a visit to the eye doctor and walked into my third grade classroom wearing glasses for the first time. These glasses were ridiculous. They were like two steering wheels sitting on either side of my nose. All I could think was how well they went with my buckteeth and big ears.

When I walked into class, some kids started laughing, and then chanting, "Nerd alert! Nerd alert!" I wanted to hide.

Then my teacher, Miss Ziese, called me to the front of class. We all liked Miss Ziese. She was right out of college, and we thought she was pretty. Miss Ziese said, "I see you have new glasses."

I thought it was awesome she pointed it out, just in case anyone hadn't noticed and had missed the chance to mock me. She said, "You know, you looked like someone to me when you walked in. I think you look like Clark Kent."*

My whole demeanor changed. I was thinking I looked like Sally Jessy Raphael,† but I now knew I looked like Clark Kent.

Our worlds are created by the words spoken to us, and with our words we create the world around us.

---

*For the superhero impaired, Clark Kent is the alter ego of Superman.
†For the 1980s talk show host impaired, google Sally Jessy Raphael.

We have the power to speak life or death. We need to be like Jesus and speak words of life.

Rejecting the Message

While writing this chapter, I fear that it will be easy for you to dismiss it. You might assume your words don't have that kind of power and refuse to be strategic about the words you choose.

Remember Dr. Semmelweis and his discovery that doctors needed to wash their hands? Most of those doctors back in the 1840s totally rejected his message. One reason was that Ignaz* couldn't explain *why* having clean hands mattered. In fact, doctors mocked Ignaz for suggesting that washing their hands was so important.

I can't really explain to you *why* words have the power of life and death; I just know they do.

A second reason doctors rejected Semmelweis's suggestion was that it seemed self-indicting. If he was right, then the death of all those mothers from childbed fever was actually *their* fault. They didn't want to admit they had, even unintentionally, caused so much grief.

We may not want to acknowledge the power of our words because to do so would feel self-indicting. We have brought hurt and pain with our words, and it's easier to just not think about it.

Another reason doctors rejected the message to wash their hands before surgery was because it seemed too simple. With all their education, the doctors couldn't

*I don't feel like typing out "Semmelweis" more than I have to.

believe the solution they needed was as basic as "wash your hands."

You may struggle to believe the key to loving people one at a time is as simple as, "Be careful in choosing your words." Doctors back in the 1840s were hesitant to believe Ignaz, but he challenged them, "Just try it. I can't explain it, but try it, and see if it works."†

My challenge to you is the same. God says our words have power. Intentionally try it, even if it's just with one person, and see if it works.

What Words?

What kind of words should we say?

First, speak words of affirmation. Everything we say tears down or builds up, and we need to choose words that build up. God tells us, "Do not let any unwholesome talk come out of your mouths, but only what is helpful for building others up according to their needs, that it may benefit those who listen" (Eph. 4:29).

You speak words of life when you say

to your husband: "I'm so glad I'm married to you. I respect you."

---

†I thought I'd share in a footnote the sad footnote to Dr. Semmelweis's story. Doctors continued to reject his message and mock him. Ignaz continued to battle them. In 1865 he had a nervous breakdown and was admitted to a psychiatric asylum. He died fourteen days later from a wound on his hand that had turned gangrenous. This, of course, begs the question: Did the doctors who treated his hand wash their hands first? If Ignaz went insane because doctors refused to wash their hands, and then died from an infection in his hand because the doctor refused to wash his hands, well, I would just like to suggest that as the plot for an episode of *Black Mirror*.

to your wife: "I love you. You are beautiful."
to your kids: "I am so proud of who you are becoming."
to your coworkers: "You are great at what you do!"
to me: "You still look like Clark Kent!"

If you do that, consistently, your words will create worlds. People will start to live up to what you see in them and speak to them.

Second, speak words of affection. God does that for us, and we need to do that for each other. God says to us, "I have loved you with an everlasting love" (Jer. 31:3).

There's nothing you could do to make God stop loving you, and he used words of affection to make sure you know. We need to let others know we love them with an everlasting love.

A pastor friend of mine told me about when a sixteen-year-old girl and her boyfriend came to his office. The girl began to cry and then blurted out, "I'm pregnant. We don't know what to do. We're scared."

My friend asked, "Have you talked to your dad?" He knew her father, who was a leader in the community and the church.

She stammered, "I . . . I could never tell my dad. He's going to be so angry and upset."

He prayed with them and met with them a few more times. He kept encouraging her to tell her father. At one point she told him she and her boyfriend were going to leave town.

My friend said, "No. Let's just go tell him right now. I'll go with you."

Before she could refuse, he ushered the couple to his car. They went to her dad's office and sat across from him at his desk.

The daughter started to sob and, not looking up, said, "Daddy, I'm pregnant."

Her father slammed his fist down, marched around the desk to his daughter, and said, "You stand up and look me in the eye!"

She continued to sit and cry.

He raised his voice. "I said stand up and look me in the eye."

My friend jumped to his feet because he was afraid of what might happen. Slowly the daughter stood up and looked at her father.

He reached out, put his arms around her, and whispered in her ear. My friend was close enough to hear what he said: "It's going to be okay, honey. I love you no matter what. We'll go through this together. It's going to be okay."

By speaking those words of affection, her father created a very different world than the one she expected to live in.

We need to speak words of affection. If that's difficult for you, consider that Jesus taught us, "The mouth speaks what the heart is full of" (Luke 6:45). What comes out of your mouth is a reflection of what's gone into your heart. So, if you struggle to speak loving words of affection, focus on ingesting the loving words of affection God has spoken to you in the Bible.

Third, speak words that point people to God. I love how, when people questioned John the Baptist and asked who he was or tried to give him credit, his response was, "I am not the one. Jesus is the one. I'm here to point people to Jesus" (see John 1:19–34).

As your life looks more like Jesus's, you will receive more compliments. "You're so kind." "I don't know anyone else who listens like you do." "You're always putting other people above yourself."

When people ask who you are or try to give you credit, find a humble and not weird* way to point to Jesus. You might say something like, "Wow, thanks. But, honestly, it's not me. It's the impact Jesus has had on my life," or "I appreciate that, but I never used to be that way. It's just, well, I guess spending time with Jesus has kind of rubbed off on me."

You might even add, "Did you know Jesus once said, 'Come to me and you will find rest. I'll teach you a new way of doing life'? That's what's happened to me."

Fourth, speak words to God about people. If we want to have a godly impact on people, we need God's help. We need to pray for and about the people God has put in our lives. "God, help them to see their need for you." "God, what do they need to hear from me?" "God, what do I need to say to them?"

And what if you asked the person if you could pray for them or with them? What if you said to a friend or coworker, "I've started praying for you consistently, and I was wondering, is there anything specific I could be praying for?" What impression might that make? One of the things I've done for years is record prayers on my voice

---

*"Weird" might include, "You know, friend, ever since I was washed in the blood of the Lamb and committed myself to clean living . . ." That is perhaps theologically true, but relationally *weird*.

memo app and text them to different people so they can listen to me praying for them.

Or maybe you're having a lot of conflict with people one at a time in your family. What if you just started praying over them each night before going to bed? It doesn't have to be long, but let them overhear you praying for God to bless them and thanking God for them.

A Plan

The easiest thing to do is to keep doing what we've been doing. If you haven't been speaking words of life, just reading a chapter in a book and agreeing with it won't produce change. This is too important for us not to do, so here's a plan that might help bring real change.

First, prepare for your day by speaking God's Word out loud soon after you get out of bed. I literally mean to speak God's Word out loud. It could be a chapter of the Bible, or you might make a list of some favorite Bible passages or verses that you want to be able to share with people and read them out loud. When you speak those words out loud in the morning, you will find it easier to continue saying God's Word throughout your day. The words you put into your heart will impact the words that come out of your mouth.

Second, do some post-analysis of your day's words before going to bed. There are sayings in business: "Inspect what you expect" and "You improve what you measure." So, we end our day with a post-analysis, knowing it will help us to continue to grow in speaking words of life. Take a few minutes as your day ends to do a word inventory.

Jesus said that we will give an account to God for our words (see Matt. 12:36), so we should pay attention to the words we speak. Mentally go through the conversations you had and ask yourself, *Who did I encourage today? Who did I build up? How did I use my words to speak life today?*

Do we really need to take this so seriously? Yeah, we do. My buddy Ignaz would tell you it's a matter of life and death.

one expression at a time

SHELLY HOLLIS WAS A YOUNG CHRISTIAN who wanted people to know Jesus. She felt God calling her to be a missionary in Haiti, so she went. She moved there to love the people Jesus loved in Haiti the way Jesus would love them.

She had no idea how hard people can be to love.

One day Shelly came across an elderly woman who was dehydrated and near death. Her name was Granka, and she hadn't been cared for in days. Shelly found her soaked in urine and sweat, lying on a little bed. Granka's family had taken all of her personal belongings and divided them up among themselves. They'd put a coffin next to her and left her for dead.

Shelly was moved with compassion, but she couldn't move Granka. So, Shelly stayed with her, day and night, cleaning her body, feeding her, praying for her. This went on for several days, but finally Granka died.

The next morning Shelly was sitting, dejected, at a picnic table outside the school where she worked. A friend sat down next to her, and Shelly began to weep. Finally, Shelly gained enough composure to get out the words, "I didn't get to tell her about Jesus."

Shelly Hollis sat brokenhearted, and she prayed God would put another elderly woman into her path with whom she could share her faith.

Not long after, Shelly walked out of her church building late one night and a man jumped out, grabbed her shirt, and swung her into a wall. Shelly's shoulder was dislocated. As she lay there, momentarily completely disoriented, the guy jumped on top of her and began to remove her clothes. She fought him off with everything she had. Biting him and hitting him with her flashlight, she finally managed to get away and ran down the street, screaming for help. Shelly opened the door of the first house she came to, went in, and collapsed onto the floor.

Fatalia, the elderly woman who lived there, woke up and ran out of her bedroom to see who was in her house. When she saw Shelly lying on the ground, Fatalia called for help.

The next morning, Shelly phoned her family back in America to tell them what happened. Her father insisted she leave Haiti and come back home. But Shelly told her dad, "I prayed God would give me another elderly woman to share my faith with, and this is that opportunity."

Shelly didn't go home. She went back to Fatalia's house and told her about Jesus. Eventually, Shelly and Fatalia walked into the ocean together, and Shelly baptized Fatalia because of her new faith in Christ.

Love the Idea of Love

We love the idea of loving people. Right?

I mean, who is going to vote against love as a concept? Loving people sounds incredible. The issue is that some of the people we need to love are incredibly difficult to love.

So, perhaps this is more accurate: we love loving people who are easy to love. I think that pretty well sums up where I'm at most of the time. I might just make a bumper sticker and put it on my truck:

> *I love loving people who are easy to love!*

Or maybe:

> *Honk if you love loving people who are easy to love!*

I don't know how many honks I'd get, and actually that bumper sticker may not be the best one for a pastor to have, but it's pretty accurate.

I love loving people, but I don't want to give sponge baths to a dying woman. And I'm inspired by Shelly's story, but if I'm honest, I have to admit that if it was my daughter who had been attacked in another country, I would insist she come home, just like Shelly's father did.

I'm all for loving people, but doesn't loving people have its limits?

Love's Limits

That's an important question, especially in a book like this: Does love have limits? Are there people we are excused from loving? Shouldn't there be an asterisk next to "one at a time" to clarify what kind of people we are exempt from loving? Would God agree that some people are just too hard to love?

If you try to answer those questions guided by common sense, your natural response might be to say yes. But if you look at the life of Jesus, the only and obvious answer is no.

Jesus loved with a limitless love. He loved everyone, even—perhaps *especially*—those who were hard to love.

His love was conveyed through more than words. He tangibly expressed his love by meeting people at their point of deepest need.

Love Expressed

One of the most poignant examples of Jesus offering a thoughtful and tangible expression of compassion is when he touched a leper in Matthew 8. If people from Jesus's time were on *Family Feud*, and the question was, "We asked one hundred people to tell us someone who is hard to love," *lepers* would have been toward the top of that list.

In the first century, leprosy was a death sentence. It was an incurable disease that caused the person to lose sensation in their extremities. Dr. Paul Brand, a leading researcher in the field of leprosy in the twentieth century, often told about a time when he was walking at night in India. He saw lepers sleeping in a ditch on the side of the road, and he watched as rats came and gnawed on their fingers. It didn't wake them up because they could feel nothing.[1]

In Jesus's day it was easy to spot a leper because they would have discolored skin and sores all over their faces. It was easy to *smell* a leper. They would have had a horrible, putrid smell.

People back then thought of leprosy as being a curse from God and very contagious. Someone who contracted leprosy immediately became a spiritual and social outcast. A leper received a life sentence of never being touched—no more hugs, handshakes, or kisses. They were declared "unclean" and forced to quarantine themselves from the rest of society. In fact, if a leper went anywhere near other people, he or she would have to shout a warning, "Unclean! Unclean!"

Lepers *never* approached people—except for when one walked right up to Jesus.

> When Jesus came down from the mountainside, large crowds followed him. A man with leprosy came and knelt before him and said, "Lord, if you are willing, you can make me clean." (Matt. 8:1–2)

Did you notice that "large crowds" were following Jesus but it became about *one* man? We see it time and time again: crowds flocked to Jesus but he loved and impacted people one at a time. It was his philosophy of ministry and the rhythm of his daily life.

This time the one person was a leper. There was no precedent for a leper approaching a rabbi. If one did, he or she would risk violence and almost certain humiliation. In fact, some rabbis of that time boasted about throwing stones at lepers to keep them far away.

Jesus was a rabbi. But this leper must have heard Jesus wasn't one to keep anyone far away. Jesus was approachable, even for a leper. Even for a leper with, as Luke points out in his telling of the story, an *advanced* case of leprosy (see Luke 5:12 NLT). The strong stench of rotting flesh followed him everywhere he went. It was like a barrier that surrounded him and kept everyone away.

This leper believed in Jesus's goodness enough to approach him, but not quite enough to be confident Jesus would heal him. Did you notice he didn't say, "If you are *able*, you can make me clean"? He knew Jesus was able.

He just wasn't sure Jesus was *willing*.

Why? Because it had been made unmistakably clear to him that he was hard to love.

Touch

I mentioned lepers would never again be touched. That's a terrible hardship because there's incredible power in a loving touch.

It turns out humans are wired for appropriate and affectionate physical contact. In fact, there is a medical condition known as "skin hunger," or being "touch starved," which occurs when a person experiences little to no touch from other living beings. If you suffer from skin hunger, you will experience depression, anxiety, and sometimes physical discomfort, pain, and even hallucinations.

Science also tells us that loving touch can be lifegiving. It's closely associated with improved IQ, language acquisition in young children, reading achievement and memory, general neonatal development, and improved geriatric

living one at a time

health. Hospital studies have shown patients recover more rapidly from both physical and psychiatric illnesses if they're on the receiving end of loving touch.

Touch lets us know we are loved.

Can you imagine how much this leper, who hadn't been touched *at all* for who knows how long, and who was considered unlovable, was starving for human contact? Even though the leper hoped Jesus was willing to heal him, I'm sure he never expected Jesus to touch him.

But "Jesus reached out his hand and touched the man. 'I am willing,' he said. 'Be clean!' Immediately he was cleansed of his leprosy" (Matt. 8:3).

Jesus reached out and touched the leper. The word we have translated "touched" literally means "to fasten onto." That's how Matthew, an eyewitness, described what happened. So don't picture a televangelist wearing a three-thousand-dollar suit and standing next to a gold piano giving someone a quick karate chop slap on the forehead.

Jesus *fastened onto* the man. Imagine the scene as Jesus grabbed the leper's hand with both of his hands, or put his arm around his shoulders, or put both hands on his shoulders as he looked him in the eyes.

On the one hand, it's not surprising that Jesus "touched the man." We see him repeatedly reaching out and touching people in a loving, lifegiving way. When he healed Peter's mother-in-law, he touched her. When children came to him, he put his hand on them and blessed them. When he healed a blind man, he touched his eyes. I once heard someone say of Jesus, "What his heart felt, his hand touched."

On the other hand, there is something surprising, even scandalous, about Jesus touching *this* man. The other people Jesus touched were not contagious. Contact with a leper was strictly forbidden. Yes, Jesus healed the man of his leprosy, but *Jesus touched him before he healed him*. Why not heal him and *then* touch him? I think it's because Jesus loved the man just the way he was. The healing revealed his power, but the touch? The touch revealed Jesus's love.

It's also worth noting that Jesus healed some people *without* touching them too. Jesus didn't have to touch this leper. He could have simply said, "Be clean." He could've winked at him or given him a thumbs-up. Jesus could have healed him without touching him, but Jesus wasn't just healing him of leprosy.

Mother Teresa, who spent decades in Calcutta ministering to lepers, said the worst part of leprosy is not physical, it's the disease of "being unwanted."[2] Someone feeling that way was heartbreaking to Jesus. He *had* to cure this leper of feeling unwanted, so he reached out and touched someone who was considered untouchable and unlovable.

What his heart felt, his hand touched.

Love's Greatest Challenge

Dr. Gary Chapman calls loving people who are hard to love, "love's greatest challenge."[3]

Some years ago, theologian William Vanstone wrote about the "phenomenology of love."* Vanstone explained

*I have tried numerous times, but I cannot pronounce *phenomenology*.

the difference between what he calls false love and true love.[4] False love is conditional—you love the other person *if* you deem them worthy of your love and *if* they meet your needs. False love expects something in return. It says, "I will love you because it will make me feel good, or because you will love me back or do something for me." *True* love is unconditional. You give it not *because* of but *regardless* of.

Expressing that kind of love is a foreign language for most people. If you need some evidence, go visit the greeting card aisle next time you're out shopping. There are a number of card categories to help you find just the right card for that special someone in your life. Take a few minutes and notice what those cards have in common. Most of them express the sentiment "I love you *because* you're smart/beautiful/handsome/funny/flexible/thoughtful . . . because of what you do or how you make me feel." We tend to love people based on their performance. We love loving people who have earned it. We love loving people who will give us love in return.

Loving people who are hard to love is difficult because it's true love; we unconditionally give, knowing we will receive nothing in exchange. It's love's greatest challenge, but that's exactly what Jesus asks of us.

He takes it further than what's comfortable for us. When you're in that card section you'll see categories for your husband, wife, mother, father, and graduate. They even have sections of cards for your mother-in-law and stepson.

But a category of cards you won't be able to find: "enemies." There are no greeting cards expressing love for your enemies. There's no market for that, but that's how far Jesus goes with loving people one at a time.

Jesus said, "You have heard that it was said, 'Love your neighbor and hate your enemy.' But I tell you, love your enemies. . . . If you love those who love you, what reward will you get?" (Matt. 5:43–44, 46).

Who Do You Need to Love?

Jesus said to love your enemy, to love those who are hard to love. So, who do you need to love?

For you it might be

the parent who abused you.

the boss with their never-ending negative, nagging nitpicking.

the bully who called you names you can't seem to forget.

the martyr who is forever the victim, always complaining and making sure you know how unfair life has been.

the spouse who is constantly critical and always reminding you of the ways you don't measure up.

the "friend" who always has to be in the spotlight, constantly tries to one-up you, and has created a photoshopped life on social media.

the passive-aggressive coworker.

the annoying relative who ruins the holiday gathering.

the stepparent who robbed you of your childhood.

the ex who broke your heart.

Who is hard for you to love?

Is there a name and face that come to mind?

Some people can be hard to love, and they're not even doing it on purpose. I think of the older gentleman who came over to talk to me one Thursday when I was sitting in a local café. I had been working on my computer, writing my sermon for that weekend. He casually put his wow-that's-really-a-grande, ridiculously large coffee on the table next to my computer, and then accidently knocked it over. Right on my computer.* My computer just blinked out.†

He laughed and said, "Sorry about that," and went to grab some napkins.

Clearly, he had no idea what he had done. I had an out-of-body moment.

I thought, *Wait, is this real? Is this happening?* Then I grabbed my computer and started to run. The coffee was pouring out of my computer and down my arms, giving me third-degree burns, but I didn't care; I was running.

I didn't know where I was running to, and I suspected it was too late, but I knew I still had to try to save my computer.‡ I attempted to pray, "Father, forgive him, for he knows not what he has done," but I couldn't find it in my heart.

Who have you decided is too hard to love?

Will you choose, in Jesus's name, to love that person?

You loving someone who doesn't deserve love from you may be the most powerfully impactful thing you can do.

*I'm giving him the benefit of the doubt and assuming it was an accident.
†"Blinked out" may not be the technical name for what happened.
‡And by suspected, I mean I knew it was too late.

Perhaps a better question than *will* you love that person is *how* will you be able to love that person? Remember, the leper knew Jesus was able; he just wasn't sure if Jesus was *willing*. You may be willing but not sure if you're able.

It's not that you don't want to love difficult people one at a time, it's that you're not sure you're capable of it.

Two Helpful Questions

We'll talk more about loving our enemies and people who are hard to love, but for now I want to share two questions I've learned to ask myself that help me with this.

1. How Has God Loved Me?

When you think of people who are hard to love, there are a number of names that come to mind, but probably not your own. Yet if we're honest, we are not always easy to love. God doesn't love us because we are so lovable, or because we have something to offer him in return.

Romans 5 tells us that God loved us while we were still his enemies. He loved us before we were cleaned up. Our stench couldn't keep away his love. We're told in 1 John 4:19, "We love because he first loved us."

That's so important. It means we don't manufacture love. The way to grow in love isn't to summon up loving feelings. The way to grow in love is to be loved. We receive God's love, we're filled with it, and it starts to overflow out of us. We don't conjure up love; we are conduits of it. We get better at loving by better understanding and experiencing God's love.

So, *how has he loved us?* Paul describes God's unconditional and never-ending love for us in Romans 8:38–39:

> For I am convinced that neither death nor life, neither angels nor demons, neither the present nor the future, nor any powers, neither height nor depth, nor anything else in all creation, will be able to separate us from the love of God that is in Christ Jesus our Lord.

God loves you. He loves you despite you. He loves you more than you'd dare to imagine.

His love for us is both the model and the motivation in our love for people who are hard to love.

2. What Would It Be Like?

What would it be like to be the one you have a hard time loving?

At the first church I served was a seven-year-old boy who came by himself every Sunday. His name was Randy. He didn't live too far away, and his parents would send him on his own.

Randy was out of control. He would run around yelling and punching. There were only about fifty people in the entire church, so Randy was pretty noticeable. I tried to be patient with him, but eventually I was done. I'm embarrassed to say that the hardest person for me to love at that church was a seven-year-old boy, but you would have had to know Randy.

Then came the fateful Sunday when I was preaching and saw Randy running around in the lobby. There were glass doors between the sanctuary and the lobby. I was preaching from the stage but also watching Randy. He stopped running, took a Matchbox toy car, and chucked it at the door. The glass shattered. Everyone was startled, and I was furious.

After the service, my wife and I marched Randy back to his home because I was going to tell his mom and dad that he was no longer welcome without supervision.

We arrived at his house—an old, run-down, maybe five-hundred-square-foot single-wide trailer. His mom stepped out, saw me with her son, and yelled, "What did that blankety-blank do now?"

She grabbed him by the arm, yanked him inside, cussing the whole time and telling me how hard her life was because of this blankety-blank kid. I walked through the door and saw a couch with a stained pillow and blanket on it. I realized, *This is where Randy sleeps. This is his room.* His mom was still cursing, and it quickly became obvious Randy had no dad in his life.

Suddenly, I was overwhelmed with the question, What is it like to be Randy? I couldn't even imagine, and I felt a flood of compassion for him. In that moment, I had nothing but love for this boy who had always been so hard to love.

I said to his mom, "I just wanted to tell you that you've got a special one here. You're always welcome to come to church with him, but we're sure glad he comes every week."*

From that day forward, every time my wife and I saw Randy, we would give him a big hug. After the first few

*She never came. But I had a sermon ready for the Sunday she did! Kept it folded up in my pocket every week, just in case. It was a blankety-blank good one too!

times we realized how much those hugs meant to him, because as soon as he saw us he would come running for a hug that would about knock us over.

When there's a hard-to-love person in your life, stop and ask yourself, *What is it like to be them?* Take your eyes off of you for a second and prayerfully wonder, *What is it like to grow up with an abusive parent? What is it like to have to deal with that disability? What is it like to have your spouse cheat on and leave you? What is it like to be a single mom with those pressures?*

What is it like? You may need to spend some time with the person listening and learning to answer that question, but as you put yourself in their shoes, loving them won't be as hard.

Who Needs to Have Love Expressed to Them?

I think it's relatively easy to convince ourselves we feel some compassion for someone we used to have contempt for, to get out our microscope and detect some infinitesimal speck of positive feelings and call it love.

But, as they say, the proof is in the pudding. That expression is very strange. Have there been many court cases that hinged on evidence located only in pudding?† I'm not sure what proof is found in what pudding. Perhaps a better phrase for what we're talking about is, "The love is in the touching."‡

---

†Is the proof ever in a custard or mousse?
‡Again, "The love is in the touching" may not be a great bumper sticker, but touch that's appropriate and wanted can powerfully express love.

Jesus didn't just have compassionate, loving feelings toward that leper. And what his heart felt, his hand touched.

So can I encourage you, rather than just nodding your head in agreement that we should love those who are hard to love, or trying to decipher if you have some loving feelings toward an enemy, to reach out and tangibly express love to that person?

Jesus touched the leper because the man was suffering from skin hunger. What is the "unclean" person in your life hungry for?

Jesus washed Judas's feet on the night Judas would betray him. How could you wash the feet of someone who has deceived or forsaken you or put a knife in your back?

Jesus told doubting Thomas to touch the holes in his hands because that was the reassurance Thomas needed. What reassurance could you give to someone who has their doubts about you?

Jesus put his fingers in the ears of a man who was deaf so he could hear. What does the person you struggle to love need to hear from you?

When Peter was sinking in the water because of his unbelief, Jesus reached out and grabbed him. Who do you struggle to believe in but have the opportunity to reach out and help?

There was a Roman soldier, a centurion, who was responsible for crucifying Jesus. He was the one who took Jesus's hands and nailed them to the cross. This centurion was the last person Jesus touched before he died. This centurion was the person most directly responsible for Jesus's death. Who could be harder to love than him?

Yet on the cross Jesus looked at this man, then looked up to heaven and asked God to forgive him (see Luke 23:34).

When Jesus died, the centurion recognized and proclaimed that Jesus was the Son of God (see Mark 15:39). He realized he had just killed the innocent Son of God. What did he need from Jesus in that moment? He needed forgiveness, and Jesus had already given it to him.

C. S. Lewis wrote, "To be a Christian means to forgive the inexcusable because God has forgiven the inexcusable in you."[5] We love those who are hard to love because he first loves us when we are hard to love.

Forgiving the Inexcusable

Remember Shelly Hollis? She went to Haiti to be a missionary. She was so committed to sharing Jesus's love that she refused to leave even after a man tried to rape her.

Fast-forward two years. Shelly, still in Haiti, was walking to church one Sunday morning when she saw the man who had assaulted her.

His name was Parnal, and he had spent two years in prison because of what he had done to Shelly. She hadn't been told he had been released, and her heart started racing with fear as their eyes met. Afraid to run, she walked as fast as she could to church, crying with every step.

She got to the church, put her hand on the door, and stopped. She felt like God was calling her to go back and share his love with Parnal, the man who tried to rape her.

I have to pause and ask, Would you go back to Parnal?

If you felt like God was leading you, would you go?

Well, God has *already* called you to go and to love. Who

is the one hard-to-love person who keeps coming to mind as you read this chapter? Is your reason for not loving that person better than Shelly's reason for not wanting to go to Parnal?

Shelly turned around and ran back in the direction from which she had come. Praying, her eyes open, she looked for and finally saw Parnal. Jesus filled her heart with compassion, and what her heart felt, her hands touched. She reached out and hugged Parnal. Shelly told him, "I have forgiven you, and I want you to come to church with me so you can understand why."

He agreed. Shelly took his hand, and they walked together to the church.

Who needs a tangible expression of your compassion?

Who does your heart need to go out to?

To encourage?

To forgive?

To invite?

To visit?

To financially help?

To listen to?

To be patient with?

To hug?

To fasten onto?

To love?

one conversation at a time

I WASN'T AROUND AT THE TIME, but some pretty remarkable things happened in 1956.

Certs were invented. Lovers of fresh breath and Retsyn, the magical green flecks in Certs, have been eternally thankful for that. Play-Doh was also invented. Originally it was supposed to be wallpaper cleaner, but kids liked to play with it and the rest is history.

Today there is actually Play-Doh cologne. No one is thankful for that.

The year also saw the first Elvis Presley record, *Heartbreak Hotel*, released; the first ever shopping mall; and the first episode of *The Price Is Right*. As momentous as all of that may have been, these things are *not* why I am drawing your attention to 1956.

In 1956, in the small town of St. Joseph, Illinois, Orville Hubbard and Dick Wolf knocked on a door. There was nothing special about these two guys.* A young married couple lived in that house with their four kids, one a newborn. That newborn was actually their connection with Orville and Dick. Dick had gotten to know the family when his wife was in the hospital at the same time as the lady of this house, both giving birth. They had quickly become friends.

Orville knocked, the husband opened the door, and Dick asked if they could come in for a few minutes to share something important. The husband agreed and sat on a couch with his wife as Orville and Dick presented the gospel, explaining what it really means to have a relationship with Jesus. The couple listened as their eight-year-old son played with his trucks on the floor.

These two men explained that everyone has sinned and the punishment for sin is death and eternal separation from God in hell. But God loves us despite our sin and offers us the gift of eternal life through Jesus and what he did on the cross. If they would accept Jesus as their Savior, they would live forever in heaven and have abundant life here on earth.

That husband and wife *and* their eight-year-old truck-loving son said yes and were baptized the next week.

The Fear Factor

I heard that story and thought, *I want to have those kinds of stories. I want to lead people to Jesus like that. I want there to be people in heaven because of my influence.*

*Dick Wolf was not the executive producer of *Law & Order*. That's a different Dick Wolf. And Orville was of no relation to the airplane guy or the popcorn guy.

I bet you do too. That's why you're reading this book.

Here's some good news: you have more power to influence lives than you can possibly imagine.

But there's not-so-good news too: the influence we have typically comes through conversations in which we share Jesus. That's actually *not* bad news, but a lot of us are afraid of those conversations and not sure how to have them, so it may feel like it. Let's just call it *scary* news.

Years ago, my wife agreed to watch someone's dog while they were away. I was not consulted. The dog's name was Porkchop.

I came home to discover a strange dog in our house. I walked in. I saw Porkchop. Porkchop saw me. Porkchop peed and then ran away. It is unusual to walk into your house and be greeted by an unexpected urinating dog named Porkchop.

My wife explained that we were dog-sitting *and* that Porkchop was scared of men. Yeah, you guessed it; *every* time the dog saw me it would pee and run.

I think that's how a lot of us can be about having "Jesus conversations" with people. Well, minus the pee. Too often, we flee from them.

We have to stop running, because influence comes through conversations. Jesus knew this. The Bible records Jesus speaking to crowds only fifteen times but having *forty* one-on-one conversations.

If we let fear stop us, we will miss out on the impact God intends for us to have. I think it was no accident or coincidence that Dick Wolf and his wife were in the hospital at the same time as that other couple.

And I'm convinced that God has *you* in the home you're in so you can bring Jesus to your neighborhood. That he has you in your job so you can be a missionary to your workplace. That the cashier checking you out at the grocery store, or the inmate sharing a cell with you, or the person sitting next to you on the airplane, or the server waiting on you at the restaurant, is not random but a divine appointment provided by God.

We don't want to get to the end of our lives and realize we missed out on the influence God intended for us because we ran from the one at a time conversations he wanted us to have.

Fortunately, Jesus can help us overcome our fear. He also modeled for us *how* to have those conversations, and we're going to learn from one we find in John 4.

Excuses

This conversation never should have happened.

Why?

Jesus's conversation was with a woman. At that time, men and women rarely conversed publicly. Husbands didn't even talk to their wives in public.

Not only was this person a woman, she was one almost everyone would have overlooked. Actually, she was a woman many would have intentionally avoided. She had a complicated past and being seen with her could damage a person's reputation.

Also, she was a *Samaritan* woman. Jesus was Jewish and had been taught his entire life that good Jews didn't interact with people of the despised Samaritan race.

This conversation also could have been missed because Jesus was tired and hungry. His disciples had gone off in search of food, and he sat down by a well to rest. I don't know about you, but when I'm hangry, the *last* thing I want is to have a deep, important conversation with a stranger.

There were all kinds of reasons this conversation shouldn't have happened, and all kinds of ways Jesus could have justified not having it.

We tend to find all kinds of reasons for why we can't have spiritual conversations. Maybe you've thought,

I can't do that because my life isn't a good enough example.

I can't share Jesus because I'm not very good at it.

I can't talk about my faith because I wouldn't know what to say.

I can't tell people about Jesus because I wouldn't know the answers to their questions.

Do you notice the common theme in all those reasons? "I." All those excuses are about *you*. And they are all illegitimate because it's not about you. *You* don't lead people to Jesus. God does.

You *do* have a part to play. You get to have conversations about Jesus. But you can't lead a person to Jesus. God does that. So don't worry that you can't do it right or don't have the right words. You do your best at your part, and God will take care of the rest.

The other objection we have to spiritual conversations is fear of how people will react. But if you do this the way

Jesus did, you'll discover that almost everyone is more open than you might imagine.

And we can overcome the fear. Did you know there are countries around the world today where people get killed for talking about Jesus but don't let that stop them? In one Muslim nation, when a certain missionary leads people to faith, he then has them make a list of anyone they know who is not a Christian. The list typically includes everyone they know. The missionary then has the new Christian circle the names of the ten people who would be least likely to have them killed for talking about Jesus. The new Christian is then encouraged to share Jesus with those ten people as soon as possible.

And *they do it.*

They must be afraid, but they overcome the fear. So that's your homework: name the ten people in your life who are least likely to have you killed for talking about Jesus, and have an intentional conversation with each of them.

We need to let our love for God and our concern for people overcome our excuses. If we cared enough, we would. I know a pastor who asks people, "If I paid you $10,000 for every time you told someone about your faith in Jesus, would you do it? Would you start looking for every possible opportunity to have spiritual conversations? Probably so. Why? Because we care enough about money to overcome our fear and our excuses. We need to care more about God and people than we do about money."

With God's help, we can overcome our excuses and our fear. And we can learn from Jesus how to have these conversations.

Compelled

Jesus was traveling from city to city, and we're told, "He had to go through Samaria" (John 4:4).

"Had to go" makes it sound like a geographical necessity. It wasn't. In fact, "through Samaria" was the one way Jewish people would *not* go. The Jews considered the Samaritans "dogs" because they were the half-breed result of forbidden mixed marriages. Jewish people would *never* go through Samaria. Instead, they would go through Perea by crossing over the Jordan. It was longer but avoided the spiritual defilement of entering Samaria.

So, if it wasn't because of geography, why did Jesus *have* to go through Samaria? I think it was because of this woman. I wonder if maybe the original plan was to take the well-traveled route through Perea but, as he prayed that morning, he felt a nudge from God. *Go through Samaria.*

Have you ever felt that nudge? Maybe God impressed on you that there was an old friend you needed to check in with, or a coworker you should talk to, or a family member you had to call.

Better question: Do you *pray* for that nudge?

I have a pastor friend who encourages his church to pray each morning, "God, how do you want to love me today, and who do you want to love through me today?" Do you ask God for divine appointments?

Jesus sought out this woman who was far from God because he wanted everyone to be close to God. We need to do the same.

It may be a challenge, because the longer you're a Christian, the less likely you are to spend time with non-Christians. Joe Aldridge has done extensive research on this and tells us that after being a Christian for two years, the average follower of Jesus no longer has a single significant relationship with a non-believer.[1] It happens because Christians spend so much of their time with their Christian friends and at church events. I've heard this called "Rabbit Hole Christianity," because the only time Christians are around non-Christians is when they pop out of their Christian hole and make a mad dash to some other Christian event.

We need to get close to people who are far from God. Why? Because we love God. Because he loves us. And because

> Christ's love compels us, because we are convinced that one died for all, and therefore all died. And he died for all, that those who live should no longer live for themselves but for him who died for them and was raised again. (2 Cor. 5:14–15)

Jesus sought out an opportunity to have a conversation. If we are compelled to seek out opportunities, we will have far more conversations.

Acceptance Leads to Influence

I was sitting at a Broadway play.* At halftime (though I think they call it intermission), I stood up for the seventh-

*In the interest of full disclosure, I have a hard time sitting through anything where people break into song without warning. But I love my wife and it was our anniversary.

inning stretch (also pretty sure that's the wrong term). The man sitting next to me also stood, and we struck up a conversation. He told me he was with his daughter, celebrating her graduation from high school. I told him we were out celebrating our ninth wedding anniversary. He asked if we had children. I told him we had three daughters, ages six, four, and three.

He smiled, gestured to his teenage daughter, and said, "I remember when she was six."

His tone was accepting and sweet. Then he asked me, very naturally and comfortably, "Can I tell you what happened to me when she was six? It totally changed what kind of father I was."

I nodded yes.

He said, "Well, I worked constantly the first six years of my daughter's life. I spent little time with her and wasn't a very good father or husband. My marriage and family were in trouble. Then something happened—a friend of mine invited me to church. I know you're thinking that church can be boring and irrelevant. I thought that too. I didn't want to go at first, but he kept asking and I finally agreed. I've never thought too highly of organized religion. I still don't. But I discovered a *relationship* with Jesus—and it changed my life. He was what I had been looking for. He totally changed my family. I've experienced so much joy as a father and husband. It was the best thing I ever did. I know we don't know each other but . . . well, I just wanted to tell you how glad I am that I made that decision when my daughter was six. It has made all the difference."

I know I should've told him I was a Christian, but I was in shock. No stranger had ever shared their faith with me before. The show started back up, and we both sat back down. I realized I had tears in my eyes—not because of what was happening on the stage, but because of what just happened in the audience. Because the guy sitting next to me found the courage to have a conversation to try to help someone else understand who Jesus is and what he could do in their life.

I was sitting in a theatre on Broadway. Jesus sat down at a well in Samaria.

A well was kind of the social gathering place back then. Women would go at sundown to get water, to see people, to chat, to gossip, to argue about which restaurant made the best spicy chicken sandwich.

No one was at the well when Jesus showed up.

Why? It was noon and way too hot to lug water around. Going to the well at noon back then would be the equivalent of going grocery shopping at 3:00 a.m. today. No one does that.

Jesus sat down, and then she walked up with her bucket to get water.

This woman had been married five times and was now living with a man who wasn't her husband. She was the subject of other people's stares and whispers. A preacher named J. Vernon McGee* said, "One reason she may not have been real popular with the women of the town was because she was real popular with the men of the town."[2]

Had she divorced all these men, one after another? Almost certainly not. In those days a woman couldn't really

*This chapter now features an Orville and a Vern. Next up? Clarence and Elmer.

divorce her husband, but a husband could divorce his wife for about anything. Whatever her story, it included five different marriages, and each marriage ended in disappointment. Each husband, it would seem, promised to love and care for her, and each husband left her wounded and lonely and broken.

Why would you go shopping at three in the morning? Maybe because then you wouldn't have to see anyone. Why did this woman go to the well at noon? She didn't want to see anyone.

Except she did.

Jesus was there. She knew that even if he was unaware of her history with men, he'd still look down on her. He was a man. She was a woman. That meant he wouldn't even talk to her.

Except he did.

Jesus asked her, "Will you give me a drink?" (John 4:7). She was stunned. Not only was a man talking to her but she could tell from his accent that he was Jewish. She was a Samaritan but for some reason he didn't judge her. Speaking to her was an indication of acceptance.

And acceptance is a first step toward influence.

When God puts people in your life, there may be things that separate you. You might know something about them or their past that tempts you to look down on the person. Jesus *never* did that, and looking down on someone never leads them to Jesus. No one has ever been judged into faith.

God told us to "accept one another, then, just as Christ accepted you" (Rom. 15:7). Jesus accepted you despite all your sin. You need to accept others as Jesus accepted you. If you do so, you might just help them accept Jesus.

Lead with Questions

Jesus started the conversation by asking her a question: "Will you give me a drink?"

This has had a huge impact on the way I try to connect with people one at a time. When we ask a question, it shows we value the other person and believe they're worth knowing.

Christians are sometimes known for wanting to talk and get their point across. Jesus was known for asking questions. In fact, in the Gospels we see Jesus ask 307 questions! And get this: we see people ask Jesus 183 questions, but he directly answered only three of them!

What if we were more like Jesus? We need to ask questions, lots of questions, because we care about the person. God cares about every detail of this person's life, and so should we.

Every question deepens the relationship and makes it easier to talk about deeper things.

Notice Jesus initiates the conversation with a very simple question. You don't have to start by asking big, personal questions. Big questions right off the bat can be intimidating and make the person feel like you're trying to sell them something.

One day I was shopping with my wife in the mall. When I say shopping, I mean that I sat in the designated husband area in each store. My wife sat me down in one store, and as I was waiting patiently, another wife deposited her husband next to me. When she walked away, he turned to me. "What if I told you that you could double your income? Is that something you'd be interested in?" he asked.

Umm, my name is Kyle. I'm a Pisces. My favorite color is black. I just looked at him in disbelief. *You really want to lead with that, bro?*

Don't start with questions that make it sound like you're selling something. You're *not*. You love the person. Ask natural questions you would ask someone you genuinely care about, because you do genuinely care. If you don't, then you have some *in then through* work to do.

Ask simple questions. Where did you grow up? What was your family like? What are you into?

When we sit down for a meal as a family, my wife loves to pull out a box of conversation starters. There are hundreds of cards that ask a wide variety of questions. Some deal with memories. Some ask for opinions and preferences. Some are personal and require vulnerability. It's true that when she gets these cards out there is often a collective moan, but once the questions begin, everyone becomes engaged.

If you don't know what to ask, follow Jesus's lead. He asked a question drawn from the immediate situation. Jesus was at a well. He asked about water. So, if you're getting your hair cut, you could ask the person cutting your hair about the worst customer they've ever had. You could ask a person at work what they like most about their job. Ask your coworker about the pictures on their desk. Ask the person next to you at the gym about their lifting routine.

Ask questions and be ready, because it will open a door to a spiritual conversation.

From Superficial to Spiritual

Jesus asked for water, and this surprised woman asked Jesus why he was willing to talk to her. Jesus responded, "If you knew the gift of God and who it is that asks you for a drink, you would have asked him and he would have given you living water" (John 4:10).

The woman was confused. She's like, "Umm, well, you're the one without a bucket. So how can you give me water?"

Jesus sensed that this was the moment to take the conversation from superficial to spiritual. "Whoever drinks the water I give them will never thirst. Indeed, the water I give them will become in them a spring of water welling up to eternal life," he said (v. 14).

When you're talking to someone, this is the point in the conversation when you might feel like throwing up. You may be nervous if . . .

You're eating with your non-Christian extended family at Thanksgiving and want to ask, "Could I pray before we eat?"

You're talking to a neighbor who asks what you did this weekend, and you realize you can share what you learned at church.

You're sitting in the stands at your kid's game when another parent compliments you on your child's behavior, and it hits you that this is the perfect chance to be vulnerable about the challenges of parenting but also how God has helped you along the way.

At some point, you'll see an opportunity to turn your conversation from superficial to spiritual. It will feel uncomfortable. Expect it. I'm a pastor, a "professional" at talking about Jesus. When I stand up in front of a few thousand people I don't know, I don't get nervous. But I do get nervous when I sit down with someone one-on-one.

A few years back, I was sitting in the waiting area as my car was being repaired. There was only one other person in the room, a woman who was reading a *People* magazine. Question: Was the two of us being alone in that room a random accident or a divine appointment?

I didn't want to bother her, but I was praying with my eyes open and wanted to view the moment as a potential divine encounter God had staged at the start of eternity. On the cover of the magazine was a picture of Chip and Joanna Gaines. I pointed to it and asked her, "Are you a fan of the show *Fixer Upper?*" She was a big fan and was more than happy to talk to me about it. I had watched the show a number of times but didn't know much about it, so I just kept asking questions.

"Why do you think it's so popular?" "Do you have a favorite episode?" "Do you think Chip is like that in real life?"

I kept looking for an opportunity to move the conversation to something spiritual. I didn't want to force it, and if it didn't happen, that was fine. Either way, I was glad to make a friend.

But then I asked a question that opened up the door. "What's your favorite part of the show?"

She said, "That's easy. My favorite part of the show is the big reveal at the end. Sometimes I just fast-forward to the end so I can see the before and after. It's amazing to see the transformation."

This was my chance. I swallowed hard and said, "That's probably my favorite part of the show too. I think it's my favorite because it reminds me of my job."

She asked me, "Do you do home remodeling?"

I laughed a little and said, "No; my wife wishes. I'm actually a pastor, but my favorite part of the job is to see transformation." And I told her a story of a guy who came to our church and who recently got out of rehab, and how when I went to see him I didn't even recognize him.

We talked a little bit more, and then . . . I baptized her in the employee break room!

No, that's not true. But I did discover that she was new to the area, and I told her about a group at our church especially for people who had just moved here.

Our conversation got cut short because her car was ready. But I got to have a conversation with her and point her to Jesus. And every time a rerun of *Fixer Upper* comes on, I say a prayer for her.

As you ask questions, look for opportunities to turn the conversation in a spiritual direction, but don't jerk the wheel. Be patient. Let it happen naturally.

From Spiritual to Personal

Jesus offered this Samaritan woman water that would forever quench her thirst. His point was spiritual, but she was still thinking physical. She asked Jesus for some of this crazy "all you can drink" water. He replied, "Go, call your husband and come back" (v. 16).

Oh no, he didn't. Yes, he did. He went there. She thought he was the one person who didn't know the one thing she didn't want anyone to know. But he knew, and he brought it up.

> "I have no husband," she replied.
> Jesus said to her, "You are right when you say you have no husband. The fact is, you have had five husbands, and the man you now have is not your husband. What you have just said is quite true." (vv. 17–18)

Why does Jesus bring this up? Because eventually you have to move the conversation from the spiritual to the personal. Most people have been exposed to Christianity but have concluded it's not relevant. We have to connect the dots and help them see this isn't about some two-thousand-year-old book that some people believe; it's about a God who knows you and loves you and can make all the difference in your life.

I've found the best opportunities to make it personal are often with people who are hurting. Pain can lead someone to seek help or answers they are lacking. I would encourage you to pray, one at a time, through the people who are in your circle of influence and ask, "Who is hurting?" Whether the person has lost a loved one, has been diagnosed with an illness, is facing financial pressures, or has a marriage that's falling apart, you have the chance to compassionately share a message of hope they desperately need to hear. It's the best favor you will ever do for them.

Answer and Advance

Jesus makes it personal, and the Samaritan woman at the well does what people almost always do. She tries to sidetrack the conversation.

> "Sir," the woman said, "I can see that you are a prophet. Our ancestors worshiped on this mountain, but you Jews claim that the place where we must worship is in Jerusalem." (vv. 19–20)

He gets personal; she gets theological. She brings up a controversial topic to try to draw Jesus into a debate.

This will happen to you too. When you make the conversation personal, don't be surprised if the person asks questions designed to take the focus off of them. Most of the time those questions are a spiritual smokescreen. It's a way of keeping God at a distance. When I hear those questions, I often think it means a breakthrough is coming.

The questions you'll be asked are pretty predictable. People ask, "How can you believe that there's only one way to God?" or "If God is good, why is there so much pain and suffering?" or "How can I believe the Bible is really true?" or "Why are there so many hypocrites in the church?" or "Why would a loving God send people to hell?"

The bad news is that those questions are hard to answer. The good news is that you're not trying to win a debate; you're trying to love a person who God loves. More good news: you're not alone in answering these questions. God is with you, and it's often in those moments that God will give you just the right thing to say.

My friend Matt Reagan was sitting on a plane next to a woman who said she was in the adult entertainment industry. Matt told her he was a pastor, and the conversation suddenly became a confrontation. She went on the attack. "Now listen. I just don't get this whole God thing. I can't even fathom why you would ever believe in God. You talk about how he's so great. But, oh, by the way, in his greatness, he allows millions of children to starve every day. That's your God?"

Matt said he was tempted to amp it up, confident he could win this debate, but instead he prayed. God reminded Matt of his own brokenness, where he came from, and the questions he had wondered about God.

He became overwhelmed with compassion, and God gave him a question for her. He said, "Can I ask you a question?"

She rolled her eyes. "I'm an open book."

Matt asked, "Are you really mad at God because of the hungry kids around the world, or are you angry because you were abused as a child?"

This woman, who had been so hard a moment ago, started bawling. Matt began to cry too. God broke down the wall and enabled a real conversation about him to happen.

When you're asked a question, pray. God might surprise you with an unexpected answer.

Or he might not, so be ready with some basic answers to the most common questions. They don't have to be extensive, just simple, honest answers. There are all kinds of resources—books, sermons, websites—that can help you.

You might even refer the person to a place online where they can find answers for themselves.

I'd encourage you to answer the question, so the person feels heard, but then move on. That's what Jesus did. He responded to her question, but she was still confused even after Jesus's explanation. "I know that Messiah (called Christ) is coming," she said. "When he comes, he will explain everything to us" (v. 25).

Jesus then turned to her and said, "I am the Messiah!" (v. 26 NLT).

It's the first time in the Gospels that Jesus identifies himself as the Messiah. I love who he revealed it to: a Samaritan woman with a bad reputation.

Can you imagine this moment for her? She just went to the grocery store at three in the morning and met God in the bottled water aisle! Her entire life changed because of an unexpected conversation that led her to understand who Jesus is.

Those are the kind of conversations God wants *us* to have. If we follow Jesus's example in how to have a spiritual conversation, those conversations will help people follow Jesus.

Come, See

I love this woman's reaction to the conversation:

> Then, leaving her water jar, the woman went back to the town and said to the people, "Come, see a man who told me everything I ever did. Could this be the Messiah?" They came out of the town and made their way toward him. (vv. 28–30)

She had met the Christ, realized he accepted her despite her sin, and was compelled by his love to act.

So she ran to the very people she was trying to avoid. Think about that. She had a great reason to *not* have this conversation with them. They judged her for everything she ever did. Yet she ran to them and invited them to "come, see a man who told me everything I ever did" (v. 29).

The story she had been ashamed of was transformed into the story she was willing to share to point people to Jesus. Her response to meeting Jesus was to help other people meet him. Her response to being loved by God was to help other people experience his love. Her response to her life being changed was to help other people have their lives changed.

And that is *exactly* what happened:

> Many of the Samaritans from that town believed in him because of the woman's testimony, "He told me everything I ever did." So when the Samaritans came to him, they urged him to stay with them, and he stayed two days. And because of his words many more became believers.
>
> They said to the woman, "We no longer believe just be-cause of what you said; now we have heard for ourselves, and we know that this man really is the Savior of the world." (vv. 39–42)

This living-in-sin, looked-down-on, scandal-drenched woman started a revival.

By the way, do you remember the story from Acts we talked about in chapter 3? If you noticed, Philip was preaching and baptizing many men and women in

Samaria. There was a revival breaking out there—but it didn't begin with Philip. It began when Jesus had a conversation with one woman at a well, and she began to have conversations with others where she shared her testimony of what Jesus had done for her.

If she can, *you* can. It all starts with a conversation.

Orville and Dick

Orville Hubbard and Dick Wolf knocked on a door and initiated a spiritual conversation with a young couple. They shared Jesus. The couple and their son put their faith in Jesus.

That was back in 1956, but today I call that couple Grandma and Grandpa. The little eight-year-old playing with trucks was my dad. Everything good in my life traces back to two men I've never met who loved people one at a time and cared enough to find the courage to knock on a door and have a conversation.

One of the reasons I can't wait for heaven is to thank them. I bet they could have found other things to do that day, were nervous when they walked up to the house, and were scared of questions they didn't know how to answer. I bet it was completely out of their comfort zone. They did it anyway. Christ's love compelled them.

I can't wait to tell them *thank you.* Thank you for the family I grew up in. Thank you for my wife. Thank you for my children. Thank you for the incredible church family I get to be a part of. Thank you that my life has been filled with love and purpose and hope. Thank you that I am in heaven. Thank you for having that conversation with my grandparents. Introducing them to Jesus completely changed *my* life.

Thinking about it, I can't help but wonder, Who in heaven is going to thank *me*? Who in heaven is going to thank *you*? I don't know, but I do know that you will have opportunities this week to initiate spiritual conversations. It may be at work, in a coffee shop, at school, or out by your mailbox. God is going to put someone in your life this week, and he wants to use you to change that person's life, one conversation at a time.

one meal
at a time

I HAVE A CONFESSION TO MAKE. When I'm hungry, I care more about food than people.

One of my favorite things to eat is caramel corn. Caramel corn is a snack, but when I eat caramel corn it usually becomes a meal. I eat till it's gone. Judge me for it if you want, but the person who can eat only a handful is the one with the real issue.

Because of my fondness for caramel corn, my wife doesn't allow it in the house, but when we go on family vacation she will usually go to Costco and buy a gigantic bag of caramel and cheese popcorn. I don't know whose blasphemous idea it was to combine caramel and cheese popcorn, but that's the fallen world we live in.

This past summer I was on vacation with about twenty-five extended family members. On the first day I opened our big bag of caramel and cheese popcorn and sat on the couch to watch a ball game. There is a warning on the bag of popcorn that says "Caramel corn may settle." That means it's on the bottom and you have to work for it.* You've got to jam your hand through all the cheese popcorn to get to the good stuff. That's what I did as I sat on the couch. Like an experienced and determined miner, I dug through the cheese popcorn to get to the caramel until, without even realizing it, I had eaten all of it.

Later that day, one of my sisters confronted the entire family about what happened.† She was sure one of the adolescents had dug through the popcorn and eaten all the caramel. There were pointed fingers and raised voices and wild accusations. My dad, who was footing the bill for this vacation, tried to keep the peace as his kids and grandkids turned on each other.

I was upset too until it struck me: *It was me!* I knew not what I had done. In that moment my sister came over and grabbed my hand. After a quick examination, she presented her evidence. There was a cheese stain on my fingers‡ from the caramel mining I had done. I told my family, "It was me. I am sorry."

My sister shot back, "Are you sorry? Or are you just sorry you got caught?"

That was a fair question.

We could have poured the popcorn in bowls and sat on the couches together eating, laughing, and connecting.

---

*Or, as one proofreader suggested: turn the bag upside down and eat in from the bottom.
†You should know that a caramel corn addiction is hereditary and runs through my family.
‡A condition known as *Cheetle*, typically associated with Cheetos residue.

We could have celebrated the fact that this was rare time we had together as family to do this, but instead the food divided us.

This chapter is about being intentional to connect with people over food. In the Gospels, we can see that instead of creating division and causing people to turn on each other, sharing a meal created opportunities for unity and connecting with people who are different. There's something that happens when we share one meal at a time with one person at a time.

In case you haven't noticed throughout this book, many of the one at a time stories we have studied involve Jesus eating with others. One of the most common accusations the religious leaders had against Jesus was that he would eat with people who were unclean sinners, outcasts, and outsiders. When Jesus connected with people, it was often over a meal.

In Scripture, God is most consistently described as a father. He is our perfect heavenly Father. He looks down at the world filled with his kids whom he loves and whom he deeply desires to love each other. As a father, it grieves him to see his kids turn on each other and be divided over so many things. Politics. Race. Social status. Religion. Caramel corn.

How does it feel to be the father of seven billion kids who can't get along? Even worse, sometimes the separation between people can keep people separated from God.

So, what's the solution for the walls we have built and the barriers that seem to separate us?

Food.

Meals Heal

I am aware of "foodies" who have refined taste and enjoy trying new gourmet restaurants and dishes.

I, however, like hot dogs. Pigs in a blanket, actually. These are a little more high-class, as they involve a biscuit wrapped around the hot dog. And not the expensive, fancy, 100 percent premium beef hot dogs. I'm good with the super cheap, 100 percent you-don't-want-to-know-the-ingredients hot dogs. A pack of eight for 99 cents? Yes, please!

So, I'm not a food connoisseur or authority, but I do know this: meals heal. There's something that happens around the table. Eating together brings people together. A shared meal has a way of leading to a shared life. One of the most effective ways to influence someone is over one meal at a time.

With a meal, there may be awkwardness during the appetizers, but by the main course we're often having meaningful conversation. We move from talking about what's going on with the weather to what's going on in our lives. We're not just sharing food; we're sharing needs and dreams and concerns. Eventually, a meal will provide the opportunity to connect with someone and share what Jesus has done in our lives in an unforced way.

Breaking Bread Breaks Barriers

In the Bible, we see Jesus eating a *lot* of meals.*

Why?

*It's worth noting that the Bible *never* mentions Jesus going to a dentist. Just sayin'.

Because Jesus came to bring people and God together and, because people are God's kids, to bring people and people together.

> For Christ himself has brought peace to us. He united Jews and Gentiles into one people when, in his own body on the cross, he broke down the wall of hostility that separated us. . . . He made peace between Jews and Gentiles by creating in himself one new people from the two groups. Together as one body, Christ reconciled both groups to God by means of his death on the cross, and our hostility toward each other was put to death.
>
> He brought this Good News of peace to you Gentiles who were far away from him, and peace to the Jews who were near. Now all of us can come to the Father through the same Holy Spirit because of what Christ has done for us. (Eph. 2:14–18 NLT)

Jesus came not only to tear down the wall of sin that was a barrier separating God and people but also to tear down the barriers that separate people and people. *And* bringing people together helps bring people to God. Jesus didn't just come to make a way for people to be connected to God but for people to be connected to each other.

Jesus came to break barriers, and one of the best ways to do that is by breaking bread.

God is a father with a world full of his kids dividing over everything from politics to popcorn, from masks to musical preferences. People take sides and then put up barriers, and it's time for Jesus's followers to tear them down.

Make America Dinner Again

Politics may divide people more than anything else in America. Friendships are destroyed by polarizing social media posts, and families take sides and even separate over which side of the aisle they're voting for.

The 2016 presidential election was certainly divisive. Hillary Clinton said half of Trump's supporters were "a basket of deplorables." Donald Trump invented mocking nicknames for each of his political opponents and speculated that Ted Cruz's father might have been in on the assassination of JFK.

The day after the election, a woman named Justine Lee had an idea. She believed in the healing power of meals and wondered, *What if I gather people from a variety of political and social backgrounds to share dinner together?*

Justine Lee was not involved in politics. She just cared about people. So, she and a friend cofounded a group called Make America Dinner Again (MADA). They would gather six to ten guests from a variety of political viewpoints to have supper together.

MADA now has dinners in over a dozen cities around America and has inspired a similar movement in England. They say MADA provides an opportunity to listen and have respectful conversation. People take time to listen and empathize, and, in so doing, they all become a little more human to each other. Participants realize it's too simplistic to reduce others and their views to a stereotype or assumption.

Do you have tension with a friend or family member because of politics? Perhaps it's not you; maybe you know two people whose relationship has fallen apart over their political views? What if you believed God's healing power could work through a meal?

For All People

I was minding my own business, standing in a checkout line in a grocery store in Los Angeles County, when the guy behind me started talking to me. He was an older man and was wearing a shirt that indicated he worked at the store.

Out of nowhere, he started talking to me about WWII and how his father had fought in the war. I was shocked when he started to say horrible things about Japanese people using words I wouldn't repeat. He said, "It makes me sick when I see those people living in our country."

I had no idea why this elderly man, an employee of the store, was saying these things to me. I thought he might be dealing with dementia or cognitive decline. I decided it was best to not say anything, so I just turned away and ignored him.

As I did, I realized it was my turn and looked up at the cashier. She was a young lady, probably a teenager. She appeared to be Japanese. Tears filled her eyes and immediately began to fill mine.

I told her, "I'm so sorry about that."

She said, "That's okay," as she wiped tears from her eyes and managed a brave smile.

But it wasn't okay, and it's not okay with God.

One of the walls that separates God's kids is the color of their skin. Studies reveal that the social networks of most people are filled almost exclusively with people who look like them.* Worse, some have misperceptions or suspicions about those of other races. We have seen this produce a boiling cauldron of discord and distress in some cities.

I'm not saying that this wall of separation is intentional, but I am saying that this wall won't fall down accidently. Jesus came to do away with those divisions and to show us that we truly are all created equal.

The Bible tells us, "There is no longer Jew or Gentile, slave or free, male and female. For you are all one in Christ Jesus" (Gal. 3:28 NLT). Many of us have grown up being taught something different, and it can be difficult to overcome what we've always believed.

As a Jew, Peter, who was one of the first followers of Jesus, grew up being taught to discriminate against gentiles. After three years with Jesus, Peter knew he was to treat everyone as equal. And he did. *Except* when important Jewish people were around. He worried what they might think about him being friends with gentiles. It's interesting that one of the signs Peter was putting up a wall was that he stopped eating with gentiles.

Paul, another early Christian leader, witnessed Peter's racist behavior and described what happened in his letter to the church in Galatia.

> But when Peter came to Antioch, I had to oppose him to his face, for what he did was very wrong. When he first arrived, he ate with the Gentile believers. . . . But afterward,

---

*One way you can kind of evaluate if this is true for you is to look at your first one hundred Facebook friends. How many of them are of the same race as you?

when some friends of James came, Peter wouldn't eat with the Gentiles anymore. He was afraid of criticism from these people. . . . As a result, other Jewish believers followed Peter's hypocrisy. . . .

When I saw that they were not following the truth of the gospel message, I said to Peter in front of all the others, "Since you, a Jew by birth, have discarded the Jewish laws and are living like a Gentile, why are you now trying to make these Gentiles follow the Jewish traditions?" (Gal. 2:11–14 NLT)

Paul said Peter was eating with them, but then he stopped eating with them. He called what Peter was doing—acting like people of his own race were better than others—"very wrong," "hypocrisy," and "not following the truth of the gospel message."

Paul opposed Peter to his face because what Peter was doing was sin. If you believe your race or your nationality is better than another, that's sin, and you need to repent. Paul's biggest issue with Peter was that he wouldn't eat with people of another race. Perhaps you need to set up some meals with people who look different from you.

If you don't have a close friend from another race, who could you ask to go out for breakfast? What if you told them, very humbly, that you want to better understand what it's like to be someone who is not you? What if you asked them if they would share their story, some truths about their race, and any experiences they've had with racism?

Jesus came to tear down the walls that divide people. If you've committed your life to following him, *you* committed your life to tearing down the walls that divide people. He came to bring peace and calls us to be peacemakers (see Matt. 5:9; Eph. 2:14), and one of the best ways to do that is by sitting down at a table and sharing a meal.

The Lunchroom

For exhibit A of how people divide and separate, go check out a school cafeteria. You remember what it's like. There is a "cool kids" table and a table where the jocks sit together, and you might also see the students from a minority race gathered at another table. Then there are the kids who can't find any group to let them in.

Denis Estimon says he never felt more lonely than in the elementary school cafeteria. Not only did he struggle to find a table to sit at, but he had moved to Florida from Haiti and was afraid to join in conversations because of his limited English and his Haitian accent.

Those memories inspired Denis, when he was in high school, to start a club called We Dine Together. The goal is that no student would ever eat lunch alone. Denis told *People* magazine,

> Long-lasting relationships are built from across the table. We want to get kids to come out of their comfort zones and realize that they have a lot in common, no matter where they're born, what they're [sic] background is, or whether they speak with an accent. In one way or another, we're all alike.[1]

Denis's idea for We Dine Together happened when a teacher asked his students what they would most want to change about their high school experience. The students agreed it was what happened at lunchtime. Denis told him, "On one side of the cafeteria, you have the white kids, the popular kids and the well-off kids, and on the other side, the new kids, the kids without money, the kids with disabilities and the non-white kids. A lot of those kids felt like they didn't have a friend and were eating alone."[2] Denis and a few friends decided to be "agents of change," and they have transformed their cafeteria.

Who has God put in your sphere of influence? Who is new, not very popular, left out, or just lonely? How could you invite that person to sit at your table? What could you do to help them feel less alone?

Cross-Cultural Connection

Dave Stone is one of my best friends. I had the honor of working with Dave for years, and I'm not sure if I know anyone who cares more about connecting with others. In fact, Dave takes trying to connect with others to ridiculous levels.

For instance, at ethnic restaurants Dave would talk with the accent of that ethnicity. In fairness, he has mostly stopped doing this, and I know it was completely unintentional. He just wanted so badly to connect with the people who worked there that he would start talking with the corresponding accent.

The apostle Paul shared that he tried to become like people who were different from him to reach those people. He wrote, "I have become all things to all people so that by all possible means I might save some" (1 Cor. 9:22). I appreciate that approach, but I doubt Paul ever took on an Italian accent at an Olive Garden.

Dave, when he finds out where someone is from, will also ask if they know another person Dave knows who is from that place. It's crazy. If we're at our local Chipotle in Louisville, and Dave discovers the people at the next table are from Texas, he'll ask, with great excitement, "Oh, do you know Drew Sherman?!"

There are thirty million people in Texas. Dave's buddy Drew lives in Dallas. These people are from a suburb of San Antonio, but Dave thinks they may know each other. It's goofy, especially when he's asking them in a Mexican accent, but he does it because he wants to find a connecting point with those people at the next table.

His percentage of body fat doesn't show it, but Dave is the most effective person I know in using a "one meal at a time" approach to influence people for Jesus. Wherever Dave goes, he comes back with a story of connecting with someone. Those stories usually involve food.

As an example, a couple of years ago Dave and his daughter went on a mission trip to Kenya. They ate several meals at a restaurant and each time asked to have the same server, Nadia. When business was slow, they would invite Nadia to come over and answer questions about her life and what it was like to live in that part of Africa. Before Dave and his daughter left Kenya, they and Nadia found an app that would allow them to stay connected. Dave and his wife and daughter have continued to call Nadia to talk and to pray for her over the app. Nadia has even joined them, virtually, for a family gathering.

Who is someone, maybe from a faraway place or different culture, whom you could connect with over a meal?

Eats with Sinners

Sinners wanted to be around Jesus. Not only did sinners want to be around Jesus but *he wanted to be around them.* In fact, when Jesus encountered someone committed to sinning, his response was to eat with them.

That infuriated the religious people. It was their biggest accusation against him.

> Now the tax collectors and sinners were all gathering around to hear Jesus. But the Pharisees and the teachers of the law muttered, "This man welcomes sinners and eats with them." (Luke 15:1–2)

They were exactly right. Jesus did welcome sinners and eat with them.

One time, Jesus walked into the town of Jericho. The most notorious sinner in Jericho was Zacchaeus, who was a betrayer of God and God's people. At the time, the Romans were taking over the world with violence and oppression. The Roman army would march into a town, demand everyone worship Caesar, and execute those who wouldn't.

The Romans would then recruit a local person to be the tax collector. In Jericho, that was Zacchaeus. Zacchaeus, a Jew, sided with the Romans and collected taxes from the Jews to pay for Rome's army so they could go to other towns, make other people worship Caesar, and kill more faithful Jews who refused. If that wasn't enough, Zacchaeus also made the locals give more money than the Romans required so he could line his own pockets with the excess.

Question: If Zacchaeus were standing in front of you, what would you say to him?

I can think of some good options. "How could you do this?" "You are Jewish, yet you're with the Romans who are killing the Jewish people. You are complicit in their murders!" "You do realize that by siding with the Romans you are betraying God? How dare you? Do you know the punishment that's coming for you?" If he was on social media, Zacchaeus would definitely be canceled.

What did Jesus say to Zacchaeus? "I must stay at your house today" (19:5).

Jesus invited himself over for lunch.

Why?

Again, I think of John 3:17. "For God did not send his Son into the world to condemn the world, but to save the world through him."

Jesus didn't come with condemnation for sin. He came with compassion to bring down the wall of sin, so he could bring people to God.

Jesus went to Zacchaeus's home for a meal, and it worked. By dessert, Zacchaeus repented of his sin and stepped into abundant and eternal life with God.

How do you make someone feel loved?

One way is one meal at a time. Breaking bread breaks down barriers.

That's why Jesus wore the "Eats with Sinners" T-shirt. He came to bring people to God and break down the barrier between God and people, so of course he was going to break bread with them.

And remember, if you choose to follow Jesus, God's will for your life on earth is the same as God's will for Jesus's life on earth.

Who's your Zacchaeus? Who has God put in your path who is far from him? God's will for your life is for you to bring that person to him.

That might sound intimidating, so start with a meal. Invite your coworker to go out to lunch or your neighbor over for dinner. You don't need to have an incredible spiritual conversation that first meal. Enjoy your time together, ask lots of questions, and listen. Then set up a second meal. Your relationship will grow, you'll feel more comfortable with the idea of bringing up Jesus, and eventually you will find opportunities to turn the conversation from superficial to spiritual.

Everything doesn't typically happen in just one meal like it did with Jesus and Zacchaeus, but you never know what one meal can lead to.

One Meal at a Time

My friend Dave was speaking at an event in Pennsylvania recently. He and his wife, Beth, had dinner at a restaurant. When they had finished, Beth headed out to leave, but Dave started chatting with someone at the table next to them. Finally, Dave walked toward the exit, where he found Beth talking to the hostess.

Beth said, "Dave, meet Leah. Guess where she's from— Kenya!"

Dave said, "Oh! I went to Kenya three years ago with my daughter. We met a waitress there and still keep in touch with her. Maybe you know her."

I told you it's embarrassing. I looked it up—there are fifty-one million people in Kenya.

Dave grabbed his phone, found a picture on Instagram of the waitress he had met in Kenya, and showed it to the hostess. She looked at it and shouted, "Nadia!"

Dave was confused. His "Maybe you know her?" strategy had never actually worked before.

He asked, "What? Wait. You really know Nadia?"

Leah said, "Yes! We worked at the Radisson together."

Beth took a picture of Dave and Leah together and texted it to Nadia. A minute later Nadia replied, "Leah!"

Nadia also texted, "We lived in the same neighborhood and worked at the same restaurant!"

That connection started a conversation. Leah confided, "I've only lived here for two months. I don't have any friends. I miss my family. I'm so lonely."

Dave and Beth invited her to come to the church service Dave would be speaking at on Sunday morning. Leah said yes and was there on Sunday.

God had a divine appointment in Pennsylvania for Dave and Leah, and it was set up at a meal three years earlier and over seven thousand miles away in Kenya.

You have no idea what God might have in store for you if you would love people one meal at a time.

So that's the challenge for you. Make time for meals with people you want to influence and impact.

I'll make a deal with you. If you invite someone to eat with you who doesn't know Jesus or doesn't have a church family, and you share your story of how Jesus has changed your life, I will pay for your meal.

Actually, a friend of mine said he would cover it, up to thirty bucks. If you visit kyleidleman.com, you can get all the details. All I ask is that you send me a picture of you all eating and tell me the story of what happened.*

*There are limits, and restrictions may apply. I don't know what restrictions, but I'm supposed to tell you there may be some. Restrictions probably include my friend running out of money and you agreeing to speaking only with the accent of the ethnicity to which you belong.

one need
at a time

OVER THE YEARS, I've become more and more grateful for the readers who finish a book of mine and reach out to me through social media to let me know how they were impacted by what they read.

But what I really love is when someone says "I read your book" and then tells me a personal story. To me, that's the test. Especially a book like this. It's not that you read *One at a Time*; it's that you gain a story of living one at a time. The end of the book is the beginning of the journey.

In this last chapter, I want us to walk with Jesus through a couple days of his life we read about in Matthew 13–15, then think through some of what we've learned together and identify some obstacles that might stop us from actually living it out.

Obstacle 1: Too Worn Out to Reach Out

You know that feeling when you go back to your hometown, or you connect with old friends on Facebook, and there's something extra special about that place and those people you've known your entire life?

Jesus went to his hometown in Matthew 13 and "they took offense at him" (v. 57).

They knew him growing up and just couldn't accept that he was more than Mary and Joseph's kid, who used to buy Skittles from the local convenience store and run around the neighborhood on his bike.

Jesus responded, "A prophet is honored everywhere except in his own hometown and among his own family" (v. 57 NLT). Have you ever felt the sting of rejection? Was it from someone you knew, so it felt like a betrayal? Usually the people who can hurt us most are the ones who know us best.

The next verse says Jesus was able to do only a few miracles there because people didn't believe in him. He couldn't help these people he had known all his life, people who must've had a special place in his heart. Have you ever wanted more for people than they wanted for themselves?

Jesus had to feel so discouraged, and, as we turn the page to Matthew 14, the very next thing that happened is he learned that his cousin John the Baptist, who played such an important role at the start of his ministry, had been executed by beheading.

Sometimes life hits you in the head with a brick. Sometimes it crushes you with a concrete block. What do you do when you're in a bad place and then receive even worse news?

"As soon as Jesus heard the news, he left in a boat to a remote area to be alone" (14:13 NLT).

When you decide you want to change, to make progress, to do something great, life has a way of smacking you in the mouth. When it does, don't forget that it happened to Jesus too, and remember what he did: he got alone so he could abide in the Father. Of course he did. Jesus lived in a vital, lifegiving connection with his Father. He said, "I am in the Father and the Father is in me" (John 14:11 NLT).

Remember, before God does his work *through* you, he wants to do his work *in* you. His influence in your life is the catalyst for your influence in the lives of others. Jesus told us that. He said, "I am the vine; you are the branches. If you remain in me and I in you, you will bear much fruit; apart from me you can do nothing" (15:5).

So, Jesus found out about John's death and left in a boat to be alone. Here are the next sentences.

> But the crowds heard where he was headed and followed on foot from many towns. Jesus saw the huge crowd as he stepped from the boat, and he had compassion on them and healed their sick. (Matt. 14:13–14 NLT)

Crowds. Always crowds.

Jesus was in a difficult place—rejected by friends, a relative just died—but crowds showed up wanting Jesus to meet their needs. You would think his emotional tank would be empty, but Jesus had been spending time with his Father. One-on-one time with God gives us what we need to impact others one at a time.

That evening, the disciples told Jesus to send away the huge, hungry crowds so they could get food. Jesus says, "Nah, you guys feed 'em." They're thinking, *What?! Bro, there are . . . five thousand men, so maybe ten or fifteen thousand people total. We didn't bring grills. There's no Little Caesars with Hot-n-Ready specials. How are we going to feed them?*

The amount of people and the number of needs seemed overwhelming. Sometimes our ability to help can feel handicapped by the hugeness of the hordes of humans.*

That feeling could have driven the disciples' thinking, and their objection may have been legitimate. But, as you are probably aware, Jesus miraculously fed all ten-thousand-plus people with a kid's Happy Meal, and the disciples were . . . flummoxed. It turned out Jesus was able to supernaturally meet the needs of people through them, even though they were fully convinced they weren't up for it.

This makes it super interesting when, in the very next chapter, we read about *another* full college basketball arena–sized *hungry* crowd on *another* mountain, and Jesus once again made his disciples aware of the issue. This time they *knew* Jesus had an all-you-can-eat, fast-delivery-take-out-trick up his sleeve. So, naturally, you would assume this time they would be all for it and cheering Jesus on, "You got this!"

*Say that five times fast.

That's *not* what they said. Instead, "his disciples answered, 'Where could we get enough bread in this remote place to feed such a crowd?'" (Matt. 15:33).

Oh, c'mon. Are you serious? They obviously knew exactly where. Jesus made bread like Steph Curry makes threes. They should be throwing up triples and running back down the court without even watching the ball go in. They should've had complete confidence about what Jesus could do, so why did they turn to him and ask where they would be able to get enough bread?

You know what I think? I think they just didn't want to do it again. They were tired. It's exhausting to distribute food to thousands of people. Loving people one at a time, by meeting one need at a time, is a lot of work.

Psychologists talk about "compassion fatigue." It's a condition when you feel distress or you feel *nothing* when you should feel compassion. Why? You've already given all you've got.

What do you do if you've cared to your capacity and your compassion tank is empty? The same thing you do when you are out of gas. You fill up.

Look what Jesus did immediately after the first *Great Jesus Baking Show.* "After he had dismissed [the crowd], he went up on a mountainside by himself to pray" (14:23).

Remember the first one at a time Jesus story we looked at together? The woman who had been bleeding for years snuck up and swiped a miracle by touching Jesus's cloak. Jesus knew it happened. How? He said, "Someone touched me, because I felt power going out from me" (Luke 8:46 CEV).

When Jesus met a need, power went out of him. When *you* meet a need, it will take something out of you.

But Jesus kept serving—he overcame compassion fatigue—by getting alone with God so he could be filled back up.

We need to do that too. The secret sauce is in then through.

Obstacle 2: Too Insignificant to Have an Impact

Jesus fed the five thousand, then got alone by himself to pray. Next, he rejoined his disciples in a new location.

> And when the men of that place recognized Jesus, they sent word to all the surrounding country. People brought all their sick to him and begged him to let the sick just touch the edge of his cloak, and all who touched it were healed. (Matt. 14:35–36)

Again, there were crowds of needy people. Jesus saw the crowds. He understood the magnitude of his mission. But, even still, he always chose to love people one at a time.

The individual stories we read of Jesus's healing feature people such as a leper or blind man or dead child. But I wonder, when it says, "People brought all their sick to him," what did *all* their sick include?

I have to believe someone brought Aunt Edna with her hangnail. Some dude showed up and whispered, "My girlfriend thinks I have bad breath. Do you ever heal halitosis?" Maybe a parent brought little Tommy, who wasn't hitting the ball in Little League the way they hoped, and asked for a special "Jesus baseball blessing."

Right? I can't swear to it, but I know people, and I'm sure it happened!

I do know this for sure: we can be held back from loving people one at a time because we feel like the help we can offer is too insignificant to make much of a difference.

One of the desperate needs I've become increasingly aware of is helping women involved in the sex industry. We might be quick to condemn these women, assuming they're in the industry because they love sin or find that world glamorous, but the reality is almost always far more complex and tragic. Most women in the sex industry were sexually abused as little girls. Some are forced in through sex trafficking. Typically, there's years of exploitation and perhaps abuse, leading to intricate, extremely difficult to overcome psychological issues for these women. In fact, women who find themselves in the sex industry in their teens will often still find themselves in the sex industry when they are in their *sixties*.

God wants his daughters freed, but how do you help a woman get out?

One morning I was talking to a pastor friend of mine. He told me there was a prostitute named Kaylee who had begun attending his start-up church. She decided to pursue Jesus and walk away from the sex industry. That left her without an income. The night before, Kaylee had met with my pastor friend and his wife. She explained she had made no money since she stopped prostituting herself twelve weeks earlier. Her landlord was about to evict her, which was especially a problem because her elderly father lived with her. Kaylee also paid for her severely handicapped brother to stay in a special home, but she was out of savings and could no longer make the payments.

There was good news: she'd finally found a legit job, which would provide enough income once she started getting paid.

But there was bad news: she would lose her home, and her brother would have to leave his home if she didn't make some payments immediately.

Kaylee asked my friend and his wife if they thought God would understand if she "did it for one more weekend." She told them one weekend could provide enough money to get through the next month.

My friend told her, "God will love you no matter what. But he doesn't want you to go back to that. That's not who you are anymore."

Tears filled Kaylee's eyes and she said, "That's what I was hoping you'd say."

They decided to trust God to figure out the situation. They prayed together.

I asked my friend how much money Kaylee needed. It really wasn't that much. In fact, *that* was the problem. I knew my church could help meet her financial need, but it seemed too small an amount. I wasn't sure it would really make that much difference.

I knew how entrenched and tangled the challenges can be when helping women who have been trafficking victims. I wanted to do more. I told my friend that our church wanted to pay her bills, and we did so, but I also expressed some frustration because I doubted that would really give Kaylee the help she needed to keep from going back to her old life.

Do you ever feel that way? When you see the homeless person who just wants a dollar? When your chronically dismayed coworker just needs someone who's willing to listen . . . again? When you are making brownies for your family and the idea hits you to make a second tray for your difficult neighbors? When the person sitting next to you on the airplane asks a question, and you realize you could turn the conversation from superficial to spiritual, but there are only a few minutes left in the flight? Will it really make a difference?

Too often the issue isn't that the need is intimidatingly big, it's that it feels insignificantly small. You can do it, but would it matter?

That's not for us to decide. We can trust God to use whatever we're able to offer. I mean, he was able to feed thousands with that one kid's sack lunch. I love this statement commonly attributed to Mother Teresa: God hasn't called us to do great things; he's called us to do small things with great love.

When I think about people who've met a need of mine, I'd wager they probably don't even remember doing it because it didn't seem like a big deal to them—but it was to me.

In eighth grade my Sunday school teacher, Scott Fields, asked me to stay after class. After everyone left, he looked me in the eye and said, "I just want to tell you I think God's really going to use you in your life. I think you are a world-changer."* What he didn't know is on the day before, my baseball coach spit tobacco on my shoes and told

*I later found out he told that to pretty much everybody.

me I was worthless. Scott spent only a few minutes after class with me. He probably didn't think it would make much difference; I've never forgotten it.

Back when I was a church intern, my wife and I had less than zero dollars. Someone came up to me the weekend before Valentine's Day and put a hundred-dollar bill in my hand. He smiled and said, "Hey, make your wife feel special." That meant so much to us.

There was the time we wanted to have our basement painted before some relatives came into town, but money was too tight. While we were out of town, our small group broke into our house and painted our basement.

A few years ago, I met for lunch with an elder of our church because I needed to share a struggle I was dealing with. I leaned in, and he saw tears in my eyes as I started to share. He stood up. I wondered, *Uh-oh. What's happening?* He walked over to my side of the booth, said, "Scoot over," and sat down next to me. I realized he wanted me to know he was on my side as he listened and prayed for me.

We have no idea of the impact of small things done with great love.

And these things make us more like Jesus. My guess is he healed Aunt Edna's hangnail and grinned doing it.

Obstacle 3: Too Busy to Be Bothered

Jesus's day continued when a Canaanite woman came asking him to heal her daughter. The disciples urged Jesus, "Send her away, for she keeps crying out after us" (Matt. 15:23).

Well, first of all, I'm pretty sure she wasn't crying out for "us." The disciples were pretty impressed with themselves, assuming that as they were key members of Jesus's entourage, people who wanted Jesus also wanted them. No, not really. It would be like Steve Kerr thinking *The Last Dance* was a documentary about his basketball career.

The disciples may have tried to send her away because she was a woman or because she was a Canaanite—*not* Jewish—and therefore was unclean and unacceptable. But surely they had spent enough time with Jesus to know that wasn't how he lived and loved. I wonder if the primary reason the disciples tried to send her away was because it just wasn't a good time. This tends to be my go-to excuse for not being able to meet one need at a time.

It's not that I'm unwilling; it's that I have a lot going on, and I can't afford for my schedule to be interrupted.

This whole book, I've debated whether I should tell you something. I guess I can trust those of you who have made it this far.

I was recently on a flight, the kind where passengers choose where to sit. The seat next to me was empty, but there were still people filing onto the plane. I knew if someone sat next to me it would be natural for us to talk. It was a long flight, and I would likely have an opportunity to talk to this person about Jesus. Typically, I look forward to these opportunities, but on this occasion, as people boarded the plane, I found myself praying that *no one would sit next to me.*

I really did.

Worse? I prayed no one would sit next to me *so I could get work done.*

Even worse? The work I wanted to do was *writing this book about impacting people one at a time.*

Ever since the epiphany I described in chapter 1, I've been studying how Jesus loved one at a time, and I've noticed something. (1) Loving people always meant meeting a need, and (2) those needs almost always presented themselves as interruptions to Jesus's agenda. If you think through all the stories we've studied, you'll realize Jesus was always on his way somewhere when he was interrupted by someone wanting something.

Once I got a call about an elderly lady named June who had visited our church one time and wanted me to come visit her at home. I was also told this woman was dying of pancreatic cancer, and hospice had been called in. Barring a miracle, she didn't have much time left.

To be honest, the timing couldn't have been worse. I looked at my calendar to find when it might be possible to stop by and see her, but there were no options. I had already committed all my time for that day. I would have just said no to visiting that elderly lady, but I'd also committed myself to loving people one at a time.

I had two conflicting commitments, and normally I would determine which commitment to keep by letting my calendar decide for me. I didn't know what to do. Should I say no to my commitment to meet one need at a time because I'd hate to cancel a commitment that was already on the calendar?

Knowing she didn't have much time left on this earth, I was convicted that I needed to cancel the appointment I had scheduled and let June know that I would "make time" to "swing by" her house. In other words, "I'm way too busy, and I'll have to leave the car running, but as inconvenient as it is, I'll stop by."

I learned that before June's one visit to our church, she hadn't been since she was a young girl. When I walked in, I was greeted by her husband, who was of a different faith. He walked me into the living room where June was in her wheelchair. I sat down and shared the gospel with her. I told her that like me, she was a sinner. Her husband wasn't sure about that, insisting that she was an extraordinary woman. I explained that the punishment we deserve for our sins is death. I shared the Good News that Jesus came to die for our sins, to take our punishment on himself. That forgiveness and grace are God's free gifts to us when we repent of our sins and put our trust in Jesus as Lord and Savior.

Tears rolled down her cheeks. She said, "I just wish it wasn't too late for me. I had my chance, but it's been too many years. I just wish it wasn't too late."

My eyes filled with tears. I told her, "Oh, I have some great news. It's never too late."

She prayed with me, and later that evening she was baptized. And she wasn't the only one; her daughter and granddaughter were also baptized.

Looking back, I'm trying to remember what I had on my calendar that week that seemed so important. I literally have no idea. I'm sure there was work and some meetings and probably a deadline; I have lots of those. I just can't believe I almost put whatever was on my agenda above God's agenda. I almost missed the chance to meet June and share Jesus with her because of . . . I have no idea.

Loving people pretty much always means meeting a need, and those needs pretty much always present themselves as interruptions to our agenda.

When you're faced with that choice, choose one at a time. You'll be glad you did.

Obstacle 4: Too Much Investment without a Guaranteed Return

I wonder if the biggest obstacle to us living out Jesus's one at a time approach is that we don't know the result. Right?

If I knew going to June's home would result in her and her daughter and granddaughter being baptized, it would've been an easy yes. But I didn't know the result, so the easiest thing was to say no.

The result we want—the reason we connect with people and act on compassion—is found in Matthew 15. It's a small phrase, and it comes as Jesus is meeting needs, one at a time: "And they praised the God of Israel" (v. 31).

What's amazing is that it was *gentiles* who were praising the God of Israel. They did not believe in the God of Israel, but the loving action of Jesus changed their minds and led them to faith.

That's our hope—that the people we serve will see Jesus in us and be led to faith. If we knew that would be the result, I think nothing would stop us from choosing to meet the needs of others above our own needs, our own agendas, or whatever excuses we might find.

The problem is that we don't know what effect we have.

As a result of our one at a time emphasis, our church has been trying to reach out to and love women who are victims of sex trafficking. One of our campuses held an educational awareness night on the issue. A few minutes before the meeting, a couple ladies who were going to attend were at a gas station across the street. A young woman overheard them talking about the trafficking awareness meeting and asked if she could come. She sat in the back and left quickly after it ended. But she somehow found the contact information for a church staff member and emailed her. It turned out she was sex trafficked.

Please take a few minutes and read some of the email conversation between that woman ("D") and our staff member ("K").

D: I wish I could tell you what it means to me that you might be good.

I do have questions for you, and I think I know how to use this in order to talk to you. I won't know what time it is when I'm gone and don't want to be traded or sent somewhere to stay. But I will be on here when I can. I need to get a new card to upload soon. I know you were trying to help by telling me to be careful of being hurt, when I tried to leave, but I didn't really listen and was hurt.

K: We understand. Ask anything you want. Nothing is off limits and I will try to answer and give you truth. Can you get a new card?

I am good, but only because of my relationship with God and Jesus, which I would love to tell you about when we get to meet.

Praying you will not be traded or sent somewhere else. If you get stuck in that—please call the hotline and let them try to find you.

D: I will try to get one when I go on my call when I get wherever we are going.

I don't know how Jesus and God are connected and who is who.

———

K: Do you want to know more about Him? Okay—yes, please get a card. Do you know if you are driving or flying? If I don't hear back from you or if you let me know you were traded, I will ask for more help. I am looking now.

———

D: Yes, can I hear about him. I am driving in the back of his van with my bag. It is dark.

———

K: I'm sending you more about God :) God made us to be perfect, to live with and be like Him. We rejected Him and did what was right in our own eyes instead of what He said. God wanted us back, close with Him, but He had to make a way other than rules, because just following rules doesn't save you or get you close to God. So God sent Jesus as a baby to earth to become human like us—so He knows how hard it is to do what is right. Jesus, though, never sinned—He is perfect in every way.

Because He is perfect, and loved us enough as His creation, He took our sin on Himself and paid the ultimate price for us to get to God, by dying a pain-filled death in our place so now we can be close to God again and He sees us through Jesus—perfect and right again.

Jesus didn't stay dead though. He came back to life after three days and makes it possible for us to live with Him in heaven after we die.

Crazy good news if you dare to believe it.

D: I am not from here so I don't know anyone.

If you don't hear from me then I may not come back but will keep this in my head. If this phone keeps safe, I can keep trying to talk.

I want to know Jesus.

K: He knows you. If you want Him to be your Savior, all you need to do is ask Him. He hears you. In fact, the Bible says He is near to the brokenhearted. He rejects the wicked—He does perfect justice, and they will answer to Him.

He knows suffering. He was nailed to a cross after being brutally beaten and whipped by people who lied about Him, but He beat death so we can too.

D: He knows what happens to me when they hurt me?

He knows the same feeling when someone whips me?

I want to know more. Please tell me how I can talk to him and if he hears me or how he can hear me. I hope to meet you all one day.

Does Jesus love me too? I think he may be the only safe man.

Do you have friends that are like you?

Do they do this too and understand us?

K: A few . . . not as many as I would like.

There are a few others—the only ones I know though follow Jesus closely.

We are planning on meeting you!

I can't wait to tell you all kinds of amazing stories about Jesus.

And yes, He loves you. He loves you more than you can imagine.

He unconditionally loves you and proved it with sacrificing His life so you can be with Him.

It's an amazing conversation and a great example of loving one at a time, but we don't know its result. We know this young woman was taken to Atlanta for the Super Bowl that year. We heard from D in a rescue mission in Atlanta. We tried to get her on a bus, but she didn't make it.

We don't know what happened, but we *do* know that, maybe for the first time ever, D knew who she was—the valued, cherished, loved daughter of God. But I don't think we will really know the result until we get to heaven.

When we connect with and meet one need at a time, we have no certainty about what will happen, but we do have faith. We trust God with the results. Results are up to him. Our role is to love one at a time.

I *do* know one result. Remember Kaylee, the prostitute who was struggling to follow Jesus out of her life in the sex industry? We were able to meet her need by paying her bills, but I assumed it wouldn't be enough to really help get her out.

I was wrong. All that happened over two years ago. I talked to my pastor friend recently. He told me he had just met with Kaylee because she wanted some training on how to have spiritual conversations with her friends and answer their most difficult questions. Kaylee is now leading a support group. She's also asking about leading a "Build a Bridge" group to promote racial reconciliation.

We don't know and aren't responsible for the results, but realizing the extraordinary things God can do with our ordinary acts of love, we need to always choose to love. We plant the seed and water the seed, but God makes it grow.

conclusion

the end in mind

IMAGINE WHAT HEAVEN will be like. Picture yourself as a new arrival. You get invited to a party in a grand ballroom. When you arrive, you walk over to a table filled with incredible-looking appetizers.

As you're putting a few on your plate, you feel a tap on your shoulder. You turn around to face a young lady you don't recognize. She says, "I just had to come over and thank you."

You're not sure what she's talking about; maybe she's confusing you with someone else. You ask, "Do I know you?"

She continues, "Well, we met once. My life was a complete mess. I was desperate. I didn't believe in God but I couldn't think of what else to do, so I went to church. I was nervous walking in. I was getting ready to turn around and leave when you saw me and came over to me with a big smile on your face. You asked if I wanted to sit with you during the service. You invited me to come back next weekend, and I told you I would think about it. I didn't come back that next weekend, but a few months later, when my mom passed away, I decided to go back to church, and Jesus changed my life. Anyway, I just wanted to say thank you. Thank you for seeing me. I came back because you made me safe and welcome."

After she gives you a hug, you spot the Slurpee machine. You grab the Big Gulp cup, believing there are no brain freezes in heaven.

As you're filling your cup, a man walks up to you, and you recognize him. He worked with you for a couple years. He says, "Do you remember me? I moved to your town from another country and worked with you. I didn't know anyone and could barely speak the language. I'll never forget the day you invited me to lunch and told me you could only imagine how challenging it would be to move to a foreign country and not know anyone. You offered to answer any questions I had, and you invited me to go to church with you."

You walk away with tears in your eyes. Nobody is supposed to cry while drinking a Slurpee, but these are happy tears.

It keeps happening, day after day, often several times a day. People thanking you for what you did for them.

A childhood classmate thanks you for seeing her sitting alone at the lunch table and coming to sit by her. She noticed when you bowed your head and prayed before you ate. You were the first Christian she'd ever met.

Someone else comes over to greet you and introduces himself. He was the young boy from Guatemala you sponsored all those years.

A server you regularly had at a restaurant thanks you for the way you always took time to ask her about her day and left generous tips. She asks you if you remember asking her if there was anything you could pray about for her. She tells you how God used that moment to let her know that he saw her.

You hear story after story of how a text you sent, a conversation you had, a hug you provided, or an offering you gave impacted people in ways you never realized.

I know this whole scenario is holy-imagination-fueled conjecture on my part, but it all seems entirely possible to me—none of it feels outside the character of God.

So let me end with my favorite part of this "What if?" picture of heaven.

One day you're eating at heaven's Buffalo Wild Wings. Your pager buzzes, and you see it's a message from God.* He needs you at the front porch.

You walk up, and Gabriel tells you to have a seat because Jesus has something he wants you to see. You sit down in a Brookstone massage chair, the official chair of heaven. Gabriel points to a road that leads off into the distance. You recognize it. It's the road that leads from earthly life into eternal life.

Gabriel says, "Watch this. You're going to love it."

You can see Jesus is standing on that road, not far from the front porch. It looks like he's waiting on someone.

Farther in the distance you see the small shadow of someone coming down the road.

---

*I highly doubt God will use outdated technology, but I always wanted to have a pager, so go with it.

Jesus starts walking toward the person, and then he's running. The two of them embrace, and all the angels start to celebrate.

It's just one person, but an epic party breaks out. As the person gets closer, you recognize their face.

Who is it?
Give me a name.
And tell me a one at a time story.

notes

Chapter 2 *In Then Through*

1. Mother Teresa, *In the Heart of the World* (Novato, CA: New World Library, 1997), 53–54.
2. John Ortberg, *All the Places to Go* (Carol Stream, IL: Tyndale, 2015), 70–72.
3. Edmund Desmond, "Interview with Mother Teresa: A Pencil in the Hand of God," *Time*, December 4, 1989, 11.
4. Ortberg, *All the Places to Go*, 70–72.
5. Ortberg, *All the Places to Go*, 70–72.
6. Ortberg, *All the Places to Go*, 70–72.

Chapter 3 The Proximity Principle

1. Miles Harvey, *The Island of Lost Maps: A True Story of Cartographic Crime* (New York: Broadway Books, 2001), xvi.
2. Matthew Barnett, *The Cause Within You: Finding the One Great Thing You Were Created to Do in This World* (Carol Stream, IL: Tyndale, 2011), chapter 5.

Chapter 4 The Power of *And*

1. "Kevin Carter," Wikipedia, accessed March 23, 2021, en.wikipedia .org/wiki/Kevin_Carter.
2. Fred Craddock, "Who Cares?" *Preaching Today*, accessed May 18, 2021, https://www.preachingtoday.com/sermons/sermons/2010/july /whocares.html.
3. Andrew Riley, "Slacktivism: 'Liking' on Facebook May Mean Less Giving," The University of British Columbia, November 8, 2013, https://

news.ubc.ca/2013/11/08/slacktivism-liking-on-facebook-may-mean-less
-giving/.

4. "Compassion," Word Finder, accessed May 19, 2021, https://find
words.info/crossword/3239166.

Chapter 6 Don't Be a Prig

1. Caleb Kaltenbach, *Messy Grace: How a Pastor with Gay Parents
Learned to Love Others without Sacrificing Conviction* (Colorado Springs:
WaterBrook, 2015).

2. Matt Chandler and Jared C. Wilson, *Explicit Gospel* (Wheaton:
Crossway, 2012), 206–8.

3. C. S. Lewis, *Mere Christianity*, in *The C. S. Lewis Signature Classics*
(New York: HarperCollins, 2017), 88–89.

4. Philip Yancey, *What's So Amazing About Grace* (Grand Rapids:
Zondervan, 1997).

Chapter 7 One Party at a Time

1. Hugh Halter, "The Sacrament of Party," Small Groups, accessed
May 19, 2021, https://www.smallgroups.com/articles/2017/sacrament-of
-party.html.

Chapter 8 One Word at a Time

1. Matthew Lieberman, *Social: Why Our Brains Are Wired to Connect*
(New York: Crown, 2013), 59.

Chapter 9 One Expression at a Time

1. Paul Brand and Philip Yancey, *The Gift of Pain: Why We Hurt &
What We Can Do about It* (Grand Rapids: Zondervan, 1997).

2. DTE Staff, "Mother Teresa, the Saint Who Fought against Stigma
of Leprosy," Down To Earth, August 26, 2016, https://www.downtoearth
.org.in/news/health/mother-teresa-the-saint-who-fought-against-stigma
-of-leprosy-55416.

3. Gary Chapman, *The 5 Love Languages* (Chicago: Northfield, 2015), 151.

4. William Vanstone, *Love's Endeavour, Love's Expense: The Response
of Being to the Love of God*, rev. ed. (London: Darton Longman and Todd,
2007).

5. C. S. Lewis, "On Forgiveness," in *The Weight of Glory: And Other
Addresses* (New York: HarperCollins, 2001).

Chapter 10 One Conversation at a Time

1. Joe Aldrich, *Lifestyle Evangelism: Learning to Open Your Life to
Those Around You* (Colorado Springs: Multnomah Books, 1981).

2. As quoted in Halter, "The Sacrament of Party," https://www.small groups.com/articles/2017/sacrament-of-party.html.

Chapter 11 One Meal at a Time

1. Cathy Free, "Florida High School Students Start Lunch Club So No One Eats Alone: 'Relationships Are Built From Across the Table'" *People*, April 7, 2017, https://people.com/human-interest/florida-high-school -students-start-lunch-club-no-one-eats-alone/.

2. Free, "Florida High School Students Start Lunch Club."

Kyle Idleman is senior pastor at Southeast Christian Church in Louisville, Kentucky, one of the ten largest churches in America, where he speaks to more than thirty thousand people each weekend. He is the bestselling and award-winning author of *Not a Fan* as well as *Grace Is Greater*, *Gods at War*, and *The End of Me*. He is a frequent speaker for national conventions and in influential churches across the country. Kyle and his wife, DesiRae, have four children and live on a farm, where he doesn't do any actual farming.

connect with
KYLE

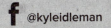 @kyleidleman   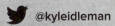 @kyleidleman

kyleidleman.com

God-Sized Courage for When You Are at the End of Your Rope

"Encouragement to keep believing, keep fighting, and keep perspective. If you need to find your courage and strength in the midst of life's challenges, this book is for you."

—**Dr. Kevin Leman,** *New York Times* bestselling author of *Have a New Kid by Friday*

Experience God's Amazing Gift of Grace

"By the end of this book you will see grace in a new light; you will see your loving God in a new light. Read it and be encouraged."

—**Max Lucado,** author of *GRACE* and *In the Grip of Grace*

Connect with
BakerBooks
Relevant. Intelligent. Engaging.

Sign up for announcements about
new and upcoming titles at

BakerBooks.com/SignUp

@ReadBakerBooks

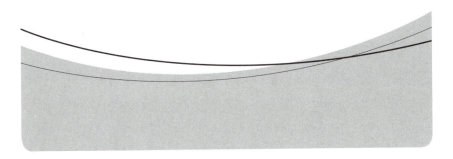